EVERYDAY Literacy

GRADE **K**

Reading and Writing

Download Parent Letters in Spanish

Each week, there is a Home–School Connection Letter to send home with students. These letters are available in Spanish on our website.

How to Download:

1. Go to www.evan-moor.com/resources.

2. Enter your e-mail address and the resource code for this product—EMC2418.

3. You will receive an e-mail with a link to the downloadable letters, as well as an attachment with instructions.

Writing: Barbara Allman
Content Editing: Lisa Vitarisi Mathews
Joy Evans
Copy Editing: Cathy Harber
Art Direction: Cheryl Puckett
Kathy Kopp
Cover Design: Cheryl Puckett
Illustration: Ann Iosa
Design/Production: Carolina Caird
Arynne Elfenbein
Yuki Meyer

EMC 2418

Evan-Moor
EDUCATIONAL PUBLISHERS
Helping Children Learn since 1979

Visit
teaching-standards.com
to view a correlation
of this book.
This is a free service.

**Correlated to State and
Common Core State Standards**

Contents

What's Inside?

In this book, you will find **20 weekly lessons**. Each weekly lesson includes:

3 Teacher Pages

Use these pages to guide you through the week.

A sample of children's expected response

A script to follow that introduces the letter and the sound it stands for

A short story to read aloud to children

Daily discussion questions about the story, plus a script to guide children through the activities

A circle activity with a song that reviews an initial and final letter sound

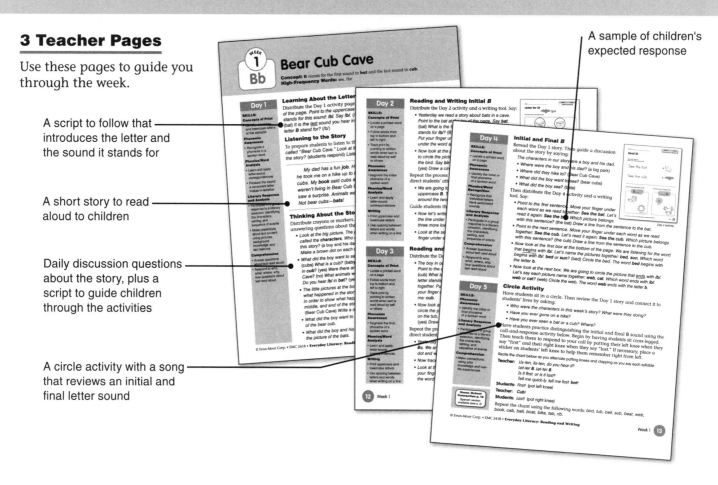

4 Student Activity Pages

Reproduce each page for children to complete during the daily lesson.

1 Home–School Connection Page

At the end of each week, give children the **Home–School Connection** page (in English or Spanish) to take home and share with their parents.

To access the Spanish version of the activity, go to www.evan-moor.com/resources. Enter your e-mail address and the resource code EMC2418.

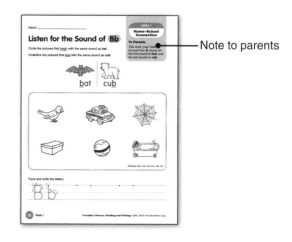

Note to parents

How to Use This Book

Follow these easy steps to conduct the lessons:

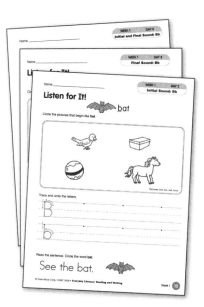

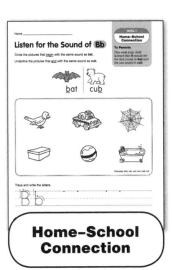

Home–School Connection

Day 1

Reproduce and distribute the *Day 1 Student Page* to each child.

Using the scripted *Day 1 Teacher Page*:

1. Introduce the weekly letter and the sound it stands for.

2. Read the story aloud as children listen and look at the picture.

3. Guide children through the activity.

Days 2, 3, 4

Reproduce and distribute the appropriate day's activity page to each child.

Using the scripted *Teacher Page*:

1. Review and discuss the Day 1 story.

2. Introduce and model the skill or concept.

3. Guide children through the activity.

Day 5

Use the questions on the *Teacher Page* to connect the story to children's lives.

Follow the directions to lead the Circle Activity.

Send home the **Home–School Connection** page with each child to complete with his or her parents.

Tips for Success

- Review the *Teacher Page* before you begin the lesson.

- Work with students in small groups at a table in a quiet area of the room.

- Model how to respond to questions by using complete sentences. For example, if a student responds to the question "Who does the dog belong to?" by answering "the girl," you'd respond, "That's right. The dog belongs to the girl."

- Wait for students to complete each task before giving the next direction.

- When a letter is shown within slash marks, say the sound of the letter, not its name. For example, /m/ represents the *mmm* sound.

- Help students identify initial and final phonemes in words by emphasizing and drawing out the phoneme. For example, if emphasizing the /m/ in *mouse*, say *mmmouse*.

- The following letter sounds cannot be drawn out: /b/, /d/, /g/, /h/, /k/, /p/, /t/, /w/. These sounds must be repeated. For example: /t-t-t/.

Skills Chart

Week	Identify uppercase and lowercase letters of the alphabet	Locate a printed word on a page	Follow words from top to bottom and left to right on a printed page	Track print by pointing to written words when text is read aloud by self or others	Understand that spoken words are represented in writing by specific sequences of letters	Recognize a phoneme in a spoken word	Segment the initial phoneme of a spoken word	Segment the final phoneme of a spoken word	Identify the initial or final phoneme of a spoken word	Isolate and identify the initial or final phoneme of a spoken word	Identify the position of an isolated phoneme in a spoken word	Learn and apply letter-sound correspondences	Produce the sound a consonant letter makes in isolation	Recognize that individual letters have associated sounds	Read familiar CVC words and common sight words
	Concepts of Print					**Phonemic Awareness**						**Phonics/Word Analysis**			
1	•	•	•	•		•	•	•	•			•	•	•	
2	•	•	•	•		•	•	•	•			•	•	•	
3	•	•	•	•	•	•	•	•	•			•	•	•	•
4	•									•	•	•		•	
5	•	•	•	•		•	•	•	•			•	•	•	
6	•	•	•	•		•	•	•	•			•	•	•	
7	•	•	•	•	•	•	•	•	•			•	•	•	
8	•									•	•	•		•	
9	•	•	•	•		•	•	•	•			•	•	•	
10	•	•	•	•		•	•	•	•			•	•	•	
11	•	•	•	•	•	•	•	•	•			•	•	•	•
12	•									•	•	•		•	
13	•	•	•	•		•	•	•	•			•	•	•	
14	•	•	•	•		•	•	•	•			•	•	•	
15	•	•	•	•		•	•	•	•			•	•	•	
16	•									•	•	•		•	
17	•	•	•	•		•	•	•	•			•	•	•	
18	•	•	•	•		•	•	•	•			•	•	•	
19	•	•	•	•	•	•	•	•	•			•	•	•	•
20	•									•	•	•		•	

Everyday Literacy: Reading and Writing • EMC 2418 • © Evan-Moor Corp.

Literary Response and Analysis		Comprehension				Writing			Week
Participate in a group response to a literary selection, identifying the characters, setting, and sequence of events	Make predictions about text content using pictures, background knowledge, and text features	Answer questions about text read aloud	Respond to *who, what, where, why, how* questions about text read aloud	Make connections using prior knowledge and real-life experiences	Demonstrate comprehension of text read aloud by self or others	Print uppercase and lowercase letters	Use spacing between letters and words when writing on a line	Write the letters that match sounds in words	
•	•	•	•	•		•	•		1
•	•	•	•	•		•	•		2
•	•	•	•	•	•	•	•	•	3
						•	•		4
•	•	•	•	•		•	•		5
•	•	•	•	•		•	•		6
•	•	•	•	•	•	•	•	•	7
						•	•		8
•	•	•	•	•		•	•		9
•	•	•	•	•		•	•		10
•	•	•	•	•	•	•	•	•	11
						•	•		12
•	•	•	•	•		•	•		13
•	•	•	•	•		•	•		14
•	•	•	•	•	•	•	•	•	15
						•	•		16
•	•	•	•	•		•	•		17
•	•	•	•	•		•	•		18
•	•	•	•	•	•	•	•	•	19
						•	•		20

Everyday Literacy
Reading and Writing

K

Student Progress Record

Name: _____

Write dates and comments below the student's proficiency level.

1: Rarely demonstrates   0 – 25 %
2: Occasionally demonstrates   25 – 50 %
3: Usually demonstrates   50 – 75 %
4: Consistently demonstrates   75 – 100 %

Concepts of Print	1	2	3	4
Recognizes and names all uppercase and lowercase letters of the alphabet				
Follows words from top to bottom and left to right				
Understands that pictures and symbols have meaning and that print carries a message				

Phonemic Awareness				
Recognizes a phoneme in a spoken word				
Segments the initial phoneme of a spoken word				
Segments the final phoneme of a spoken word				

Phonics/Word Analysis				
Learns and applies letter-sound correspondences				
Produces the sound a consonant letter makes in isolation				

Comprehension				
Responds to *who, what, where, why, how* questions about text read aloud				
Makes connections using prior knowledge and real-life experiences				

Writing				
Prints uppercase and lowercase letters				
Uses spacing between letters and words when writing on a line				

Everyday Literacy
Reading and Writing

Students' Names:

Small Group Record Sheet

Write dates and comments about students' performance each week.

Week	Title	Comments
1	Initial and Final Bb	
2	Initial and Final Ff	
3	Initial and Final Gg	
4	Review Bb, Ff, Gg	
5	Initial and Final Ss	
6	Initial and Final Ll	
7	Initial and Final Mm	
8	Review Ss, Ll, Mm	
9	Initial and Final Dd	
10	Initial and Final Nn	
11	Initial and Final Tt	
12	Review Dd, Nn, Tt	
13	Initial Jj (no final sound)	
14	Initial and Final Kk	
15	Initial and Final Rr	
16	Review Jj, Kk, Rr	
17	Initial Hh (no final sound)	
18	Initial and Final Pp	
19	Initial Ww (no final sound)	
20	Review Hh, Pp, Ww	

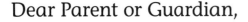

Dear Parent or Guardian,

Every week your child will complete reading and writing activities that focus on a letter of the alphabet and the sound it makes. Your child will practice listening for words that begin or end with the weekly letter and writing both the uppercase and lowercase forms of the letter. The activities provide fun practice with beginning reading and writing skills.

At the end of each week, I will send home an activity page for you to complete with your child. The activity page includes a listening activity and a writing activity for you and your child to do together.

Sincerely,

Estimado padre o tutor:

Cada semana su niño(a) realizará actividades de lectura y escritura basadas en una letra del alfabeto y en el sonido que representa. Su niño(a) practicará a reconocer palabras leídas en voz alta que comienzan y terminan con la letra semanal. También aprenderá a escribir las formas mayúscula y minúscula de cada letra. Estas actividades le permitirán divertirse mientras practica sus habilidades iniciales de lectura y escritura.

Al final de cada semana, le enviaré una hoja de actividades para que la complete en casa con su niño(a). La hoja de actividades incluye una actividad de lectura en voz alta y una de escritura, y ambas deben ser completadas por usted y su niño(a).

Sinceramente,

Bear Cub Cave

Concept: B stands for the first sound in **bat** and the last sound in **cub**.
High-Frequency Words: see, the

Day 1

SKILLS:
Concepts of Print
• Identify uppercase and lowercase letters of the alphabet

Phonemic Awareness
• Recognize a phoneme in a spoken word

Phonics/Word Analysis
• Learn and apply letter-sound correspondences
• Produce the sound a consonant letter makes in isolation

Literary Response and Analysis
• Participate in a group response to a literary selection, identifying the characters, setting, and sequence of events
• Make predictions about text content using pictures, background knowledge, and text features

Comprehension
• Answer questions about text read aloud
• Respond to *who, what, where, why, how* questions about text read aloud

Learning About the Letter *Bb*

Distribute the Day 1 activity page. Say: *This week's letter is **B**. Find **B** at the top of the page. Point to the uppercase **B**. Now point to the lowercase **b**. The letter **B** stands for this sound: /b/. Say /b/.* (/b/) *It is the first sound you hear in **bat**. Say **bat**.* (bat) *It is the <u>last</u> sound you hear in **cub**. Say **cub**.* (cub) *What sound does the letter **B** stand for?* (/b/)

Listening to the Story

To prepare students to listen to the story, say: *I am going to read you a story called "Bear Cub Cave." Look at the picture. What do you think happens in the story?* (students respond) *Listen for the /b/ sound as I read the story.*

---

*My dad has a fun **job**. He is a park ranger at a **big** park. One day he took me on a hike up to **Bear Cub** Cave. I wanted to see some bear cubs. My **book** said cubs are **born** in a cave. But Dad said that bears weren't living in Bear Cub Cave anymore. When we got to the cave, we saw a surprise. Animals were inside. Can you guess what they were? Not bear cubs—**bats**!*

Thinking About the Story

Distribute crayons or markers. Guide students in answering questions about the story. Say:

• *Look at the big picture. The people in a story are called the **characters**. Who are the characters in this story?* (a boy and his dad who is a park ranger) *Make a brown dot on each character's hat.*

• *What did the boy want to see at Bear Cub Cave?* (cubs) *What is a cub?* (baby bear) *Do you hear /b/ in **cub**?* (yes) *Were there any cubs at Bear Cub Cave?* (no) *What animals were in the cave?* (bats) *Do you hear /b/ in **bat**?* (yes) *Circle a bat.*

• *The little pictures at the bottom of the page show what happened in the story. Let's put the pictures in order to show what happened at the beginning, middle, and end of the story. Where did the boy and his father hike to?* (Bear Cub Cave) *Write a number **1** under the picture of them hiking.*

• *What did the boy want to see?* (a bear cub) *Write a number **2** under the picture of the bear cub.*

• *What did the boy and his dad see in Bear Cub Cave?* (bats) *Write **3** under the picture of the bats.*

Day 1 picture

SKILLS:
Concepts of Print
- Locate a printed word on a page
- Follow words from top to bottom and left to right
- Track print by pointing to written words when text is read aloud by self or others

Phonemic Awareness
- Segment the initial phoneme of a spoken word

Phonics/Word Analysis
- Learn and apply letter-sound correspondences

Writing
- Print uppercase and lowercase letters
- Use spacing between letters and words when writing on a line

Reading and Writing Initial *B*

Distribute the Day 2 activity and a writing tool. Say:

- *Yesterday we read a story about bats in a cave. Point to the bat at the top of the page. Say **bat**. (bat) What is the first sound in **bat**? (/b/) What letter stands for /b/? (B) Let's read the word **bat** together. Put your finger under the letter **b**. Move your finger under the word as you read it with me: **bat**.*

- *Now look at the pictures in the box. We're going to circle the pictures that <u>begin</u> with /b/. Point to the bird. Say **bird**. (bird) Does **bird** begin with /b/? (yes) Draw a circle around the bird.*

Repeat the process for the remaining pictures. Then direct students' attention to the next task. Say:

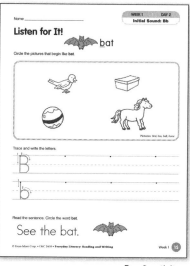

Day 2 activity

- *We are going to write uppercase **B** and lowercase **b**. Start at the black dot on uppercase **B**. Trace the line down. Go to the black dot again. Trace the line around the two curves. Go to the next black dot. Write another uppercase **B**.*

Guide students through writing two more uppercase Bs. Then say:

- *Now let's write lowercase **b**. Start at the black dot. Trace the line down. Go to the line under the number 2. Follow the line around to make a circle. Now write three more lowercase **b**'s.*

- *Look at the sentence at the bottom of the page. It says **See the bat**. Move your finger under each word as you read it with me: **See the bat**. Circle the word **bat**.*

SKILLS:
Concepts of Print
- Locate a printed word on a page
- Follow words from top to bottom and left to right
- Track print by pointing to written words when text is read aloud by self or others

Phonemic Awareness
- Segment the final phoneme of a spoken word

Phonics/Word Analysis
- Learn and apply letter-sound correspondences

Writing
- Print uppercase and lowercase letters
- Use spacing between letters and words when writing on a line

Reading and Writing Final *B*

Distribute the Day 3 activity and a writing tool. Say:

- *The boy in our story wanted to see a bear cub. Point to the cub at the top of the page. Say **cub**. (cub) What is the <u>last</u> sound in **cub**? (/b/) What letter stands for /b/? (B) Let's read the word **cub** together. Put your finger under the letter **c**. Move your finger under the word as you read it with me: **cub**.*

- *Now look at the pictures in the box. We're going to circle the pictures that <u>end</u> with /b/. Put your finger on the tub. Say **tub**. (tub) Does **tub** end with /b/? (yes) Draw a circle around the tub.*

Repeat the process for the remaining pictures. Then direct students' attention to the next task. Say:

Day 3 activity

- *Yesterday we followed the dots and the arrows to write uppercase and lowercase **B**s. We are going to do it again today. Trace the uppercase **B**. Then start at each dot and write an uppercase **B**.*

- *Now trace the lowercase **b**. Then start at each dot and write a lowercase **b**.*

- *Look at the sentence at the bottom of the page. It says **See the cub**. Move your finger under each word as you read it with me: **See the cub**. Circle the word **cub**.*

Day 4

SKILLS:

Concepts of Print
• Locate a printed word on a page

Phonemic Awareness
• Identify the initial or final phoneme of a spoken word

Phonics/Word Recognition
• Recognize that individual letters have associated sounds

Literary Response and Analysis
• Participate in a group response to a literary selection, identifying the characters, setting, and sequence of events

Comprehension
• Answer questions about text read aloud
• Respond to *who, what, where, why, how* questions about text read aloud

Initial and Final *B*

Reread the Day 1 story. Then guide a discussion about the story by saying:

> *The characters in our story are a boy and his dad.*
> • *Where were the boy and his dad?* (a big park)
> • *Where did they hike to?* (Bear Cub Cave)
> • *What did the boy want to see?* (bear cubs)
> • *What did the boy see?* (bats)

Then distribute the Day 4 activity and a writing tool. Say:

> • *Point to the first sentence. Move your finger under each word as we read together:* **See the bat**. *Let's read it again:* **See the bat**. *Which picture belongs with this sentence?* (the bat) *Draw a line from the sentence to the bat.*
>
> • *Point to the next sentence. Move your finger under each word as we read together:* **See the cub**. *Let's read it again:* **See the cub**. *Which picture belongs with this sentence?* (the cub) *Draw a line from the sentence to the cub.*
>
> • *Now look at the first box at the bottom of the page. We are listening for the word that begins with /b/. Let's name the pictures together:* **bed, sun**. *Which word begins with /b/:* **bed** *or* **sun**? (bed) *Circle the bed. The word* **bed** *begins with the letter* **b**.
>
> • *Now look at the next box. We are going to circle the picture that ends with /b/. Let's say each picture name together:* **web, cat**. *Which word ends with /b/:* **web** *or* **cat**? (web) *Circle the web. The word* **web** *ends with the letter* **b**.

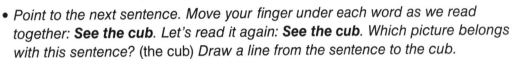

Day 4 activity

Day 5

SKILLS:

Phonemic Awareness
• Identify the initial or final phoneme of a spoken word

Literary Response and Analysis
• Participate in a group response to a literary selection, identifying the characters, setting, and sequence of events

Comprehension
• Make connections using prior knowledge and real-life experiences

Home–School Connection p. 18
Spanish version available (see p. 2)

Circle Activity

Have students sit in a circle. Then review the Day 1 story and connect it to students' lives by asking:

> • *Who were the characters in this week's story? What were they doing?*
> • *Have you ever gone on a hike?*
> • *Have you ever seen a bat or a cub? Where?*

Have students practice distinguishing the initial and final **B** sound using the call-and-response activity below. Begin by having students sit cross-legged. Then teach them to respond to your call by patting their left knee when they say "first" and their right knee when they say "last." If necessary, place a sticker on students' left knee to help them remember right from left.

Recite the chant below as you alternate patting knees and clapping as you say each syllable.

Teacher: *Lis-ten, lis-ten, do you hear it?*
Let-ter **B**. *Let-ter* **B**.
Is it first, or is it last?
Tell me quick-ly, tell me fast: **bat**!

Students: *First!* (pat left knee)

Teacher: *Cub!*

Students: *Last!* (pat right knee)

Repeat the chant using the following words: *bird, tub, bell, sub, bear, web, book, cab, ball, boat, bike, tab, rib.*

Name _____

Bb

Bear Cub Cave

Number the pictures in order.

Everyday Literacy: Reading and Writing • EMC 2418 • © Evan-Moor Corp.

Name _____

Listen for It!

 <u>b</u>at

Circle the pictures that begin like **bat**.

Pictures: *bird, box, ball, horse*

Trace and write the letters.

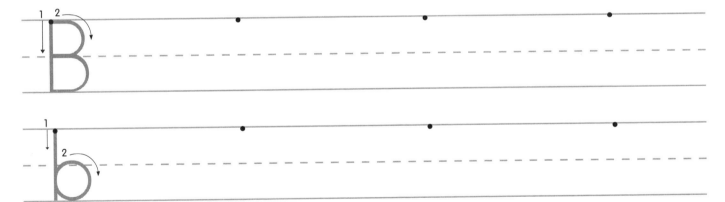

Read the sentence. Circle the word **bat**.

See the bat.

Listen for It!

 cub

Circle the pictures that <u>end</u> like **cub**.

Pictures: *tub, house, cab, web*

Trace and write the letters.

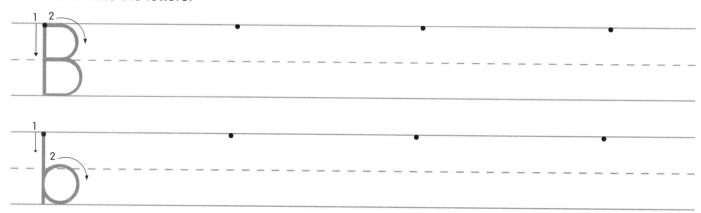

Read the sentence. Circle the word **cub**.

See the cub.

Name _____

Read It!

Read each sentence.
Draw a line to the correct picture.

See the bat.

★

See the cub.

★

Circle the picture that begins with **/b/**.

b____

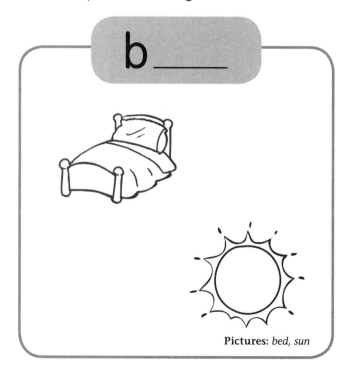

Pictures: *bed, sun*

Circle the picture that <u>ends</u> with **/b/**.

____b

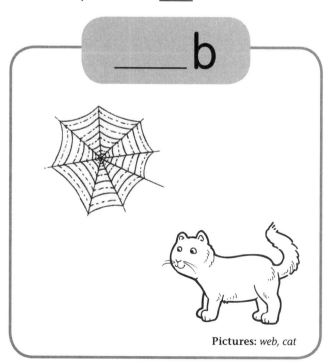

Pictures: *web, cat*

Name _____

Listen for the Sound of Bb

Circle the pictures that <u>begin</u> with the same sound as **bat**.

Underline the pictures that <u>end</u> with the same sound as **cub**.

WEEK 1

Home–School Connection

To Parents

This week your child learned that **B** stands for the first sound in **bat** and the last sound in **cub**.

bat | cub

Pictures: *bird, cab, web, box, ball, tub*

Trace and write the letters.

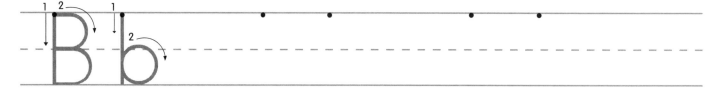

On the Farm

WEEK 2 Ff

Concept: **F** stands for the first sound in **fish** and the last sound in **calf**.
High-Frequency Words: a, here, is

Day 1

SKILLS:

Concepts of Print

• Identify uppercase and lowercase letters of the alphabet

Phonemic Awareness

• Recognize a phoneme in a spoken word

Phonics/Word Analysis

• Learn and apply letter-sound correspondences

• Produce the sound a consonant letter makes in isolation

Literary Response and Analysis

• Participate in a group response to a literary selection, identifying the characters, setting, and sequence of events

• Make predictions about text content using pictures, background knowledge, and text features

Comprehension

• Answer questions about text read aloud

• Respond to *who, what, where, why, how* questions about text read aloud

Learning About the Letter *Ff*

Distribute the Day 1 activity page. Say: *This week's letter is* **F**. *Find* **F** *at the top of the page. Point to the uppercase* **F**. *Now point to the lowercase* **f**. *The letter* **F** *stands for this sound: /f/. Say /f/. (/f/) It is the first sound you hear in* **fish**. *Say* **fish**. *(fish) It is the* <u>last</u> *sound you hear in* **calf**. *Say* **calf**. *(calf) What sound does the letter* **F** *stand for? (/f/)*

Listening to the Story

To prepare students to listen to the story, say: *I am going to read you a story. The title is "On the Farm." Look at the picture. What do you think happens in the story? (students respond) Listen for the /f/ sound as I read the story.*

    I like living on a **farm** *because there's a lot of* **fun stuff** *to do. Early in the morning, Dad and I walk down to the lake and* **fish**. *One time I caught two blue fish! On sunny days, I climb up onto the tractor and help my dad plow the* **fields**. *I also help him* **fix** *things. Last summer I helped him fix a broken* **fence**. *My* **favorite** *thing to do is play with the animals. I like the baby* **calf** *the best. I stand at the fence and pet it. Sometimes it likes to lick and* **sniff** *my hand. Its tongue* **feels** *wet and rough and it tickles my hand, but I like it. Living on a farm is fun!*

Thinking About the Story

Distribute crayons or markers. Guide students in answering questions about the story. Say:

Day 1 picture

• *What is the title of the story? (On the Farm) Do you hear /f/ in* **farm***? (yes)*

• *Look at the big picture. Why does the girl like living on a farm? (There's a lot of fun stuff to do.) Make a green dot on the girl.*

• *What is a calf? (baby cow) Do you hear /f/ in* **calf***? (yes) Draw a line under the calf.*

• *The little pictures at the bottom of the page show us what the girl does on the farm. What did the girl tell us about first? (fishing) Write* **1** *under the picture.*

• *Next, the girl told us how she helps her dad. Which picture shows something the girl does to help her dad? (riding tractor to plow fields) Write* **2** *under the picture.*

• *Which picture show the girl's favorite thing to do? (petting the calf) Write* **3** *under the picture.*

SKILLS:

Concepts of Print

- Locate a printed word on a page
- Follow words from top to bottom and left to right
- Track print by pointing to written words when text is read aloud by self or others

Phonemic Awareness

- Segment the initial phoneme of a spoken word

Phonics/Word Analysis

- Learn and apply letter-sound correspondences

Writing

- Print uppercase and lowercase letters
- Use spacing between letters and words when writing on a line

Reading and Writing Initial *F*

Distribute the Day 2 activity and a writing tool. Say:

- *Yesterday we read a story about a girl who likes to fish. Point to the fish at the top of the page. Say* **fish**. *(fish) What is the first sound in* **fish***? (/f/) What letter stands for /f/? (F) Let's read the word* **fish** *together. Put your finger under the letter* **f**. *Move your finger under the word as you read it with me:* **fish**.

- *Now look at the pictures in the box. We're going to circle the pictures that* begin with */f/. Point to the fox. Say* **fox**. *(fox) Does* **fox** *begin with /f/? (yes) Draw a circle around the fox.*

Repeat the process for the remaining pictures. Then direct students' attention to the next task. Say:

Day 2 activity

- *We are going to write uppercase* **F** *and lowercase* **f**. *Start at the black dot on uppercase* **F**. *Trace the line down. Go to the black dot again. Trace the line across. Then trace the last line across. Go to the next black dot. Write another uppercase* **F**.

Guide students through writing two more uppercase Fs. Then say:

- *Now let's write lowercase* **f**. *Start at the black dot. Trace the line around and down. Go to the last line. Trace it across. Now write three more lowercase* **f***'s.*

- *Look at the sentence at the bottom of the page. It says* **Here is a fish**. *Move your finger under each word as you read it with me:* **Here is a fish**. *Circle the word* **fish**.

SKILLS:

Concepts of Print

- Locate a printed word on a page
- Follow words from top to bottom and left to right
- Track print by pointing to written words when text is read aloud by self or others

Phonemic Awareness

- Segment the final phoneme of a spoken word

Phonics/Word Analysis

- Learn and apply letter-sound correspondences

Writing

- Print uppercase and lowercase letters
- Use spacing between letters and words when writing on a line

Reading and Writing Final *F*

Distribute the Day 3 activity and a writing tool. Say:

- *The girl in our story liked to pet her calf. Point to the calf at the top of the page. Say* **calf**. *(calf) What is the* last *sound in* **calf***? (/f/) What letter stands for /f/? (F) Let's read the word* **calf** *together. Put your finger under the letter* **c**. *Move your finger under the word as you read it with me:* **calf**.

- *Now look at the pictures in the box. We're going to circle the pictures that* end *with /f/. Put your finger on the leaf. Say* **leaf**. *(leaf) Does* **leaf** *end with /f/? (yes) Draw a circle around the leaf.*

Repeat the process for the remaining pictures. Then direct students' attention to the next task. Say:

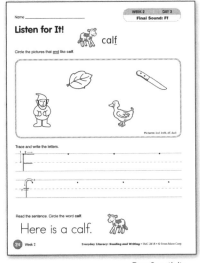

Day 3 activity

- *Yesterday we followed the dots and the arrows to write uppercase and lowercase* **F***s. We are going to do it again today. Trace the uppercase* **F**. *Then start at each dot and write an uppercase* **F**.

- *Now trace the lowercase* **f**. *Then start at each dot and write a lowercase* **f**.

- *Look at the sentence at the bottom of the page. It says* **Here is a calf**. *Move your finger under each word as you read it with me:* **Here is a calf**. *Circle the word* **calf**.

SKILLS:

Concepts of Print

• Locate a printed word on a page

Phonemic Awareness

• Identify the initial or final phoneme of a spoken word

Phonics/Word Recognition

• Recognize that individual letters have associated sounds

Literary Response and Analysis

• Participate in a group response to a literary selection, identifying the characters, setting, and sequence of events

Comprehension

• Answer questions about text read aloud

• Respond to *who, what, where, why, how* questions about text read aloud

Initial and Final *F*

Reread the Day 1 story. Then guide a discussion about the story by saying:

Our story is about a girl who lives on a farm.

• *What does the girl do early in the morning?* (walks to the lake to fish)

• *What does the girl do on sunny days?* (climbs onto the tractor and helps her dad plow the fields)

Then distribute the Day 4 activity and a writing tool. Say:

Day 4 activity

• *Point to the first sentence. Move your finger under each word as we read together:* **Here is a fish.** *Let's read it again:* **Here is a fish.** *Which picture belongs with this sentence?* (the fish) *Draw a line from the sentence to the fish.*

• *Point to the next sentence. Move your finger under each word as we read together:* **Here is a calf.** *Let's read it again:* **Here is a calf.** *Which picture belongs with this sentence?* (the calf) *Draw a line from the sentence to the calf.*

• *Now look at the first box at the bottom of the page. We are going to circle the picture that begins with /f/. Let's say each picture name together:* **cat, fan.** *Which word begins with /f/:* **cat** *or* **fan**? (fan) *Circle the fan. The word* **fan** *begins with the letter* **f.**

• *Now look at the next box. We are going to circle the picture that ends with /f/. Let's say each picture name together:* **leaf, pig.** *Which word ends with /f/:* **leaf** *or* **pig**? (leaf) *Circle the leaf. The word* **leaf** *ends with the letter* **f.**

SKILLS:

Phonemic Awareness

• Identify the initial or final phoneme of a spoken word

Literary Response and Analysis

• Participate in a group response to a literary selection, identifying the characters, setting, and sequence of events

Comprehension

• Make connections using prior knowledge and real-life experiences

Home–School Connection p. 26
Spanish version available (see p. 2)

Circle Activity

Have students sit in a circle. Then review the Day 1 story and connect it to students' lives by asking:

• *What was the title of the story?*

• *What kind of fun would you like to have on a farm?*

Have students practice distinguishing the initial and final **F** sound using the call-and-response activity below. Begin by having students sit cross-legged. Then teach them to respond to your call by patting their left knee when they say "first" and their right knee when they say "last." If necessary, place a sticker on students' left knee to help them remember right from left.

Recite the chant below as you alternate patting knees and clapping as you say each syllable.

Teacher: *Lis-ten, lis-ten, do you hear it?*
Let-ter **F.** *Let-ter* **F.**
Is it first, or is it last?
Tell me quick-ly, tell me fast: **fish**!

Students: *First!* (pat left knee)

Teacher: *Calf!*

Students: *Last!* (pat right knee)

Repeat the chant using the following words: *farm, field, fence, fix, stuff, sniff, leaf.*

Name _____

Ff

On the Farm

Number the pictures in order.

Everyday Literacy: Reading and Writing • EMC 2418 • © Evan-Moor Corp.

Name _____

Listen for It!

 _fish

Circle the pictures that begin like **fish**.

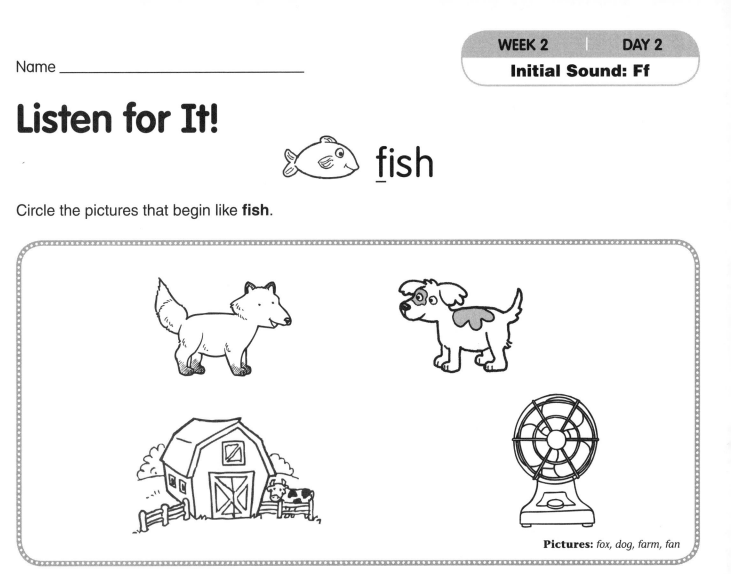

Pictures: *fox, dog, farm, fan*

Trace and write the letters.

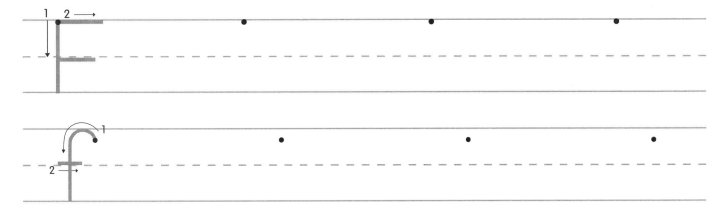

Read the sentence. Circle the word **fish**.

Here is a fish.

Listen for It!

 calf

Circle the pictures that <u>end</u> like **calf**.

Pictures: *leaf, knife, elf, duck*

Trace and write the letters.

Read the sentence. Circle the word **calf**.

Here is a calf.

Name _____

Read It!

Read each sentence.
Draw a line to the correct picture.

Here is a fish.

★

Here is a calf.

★

Circle the picture that begins with /**f**/.

f_____

Pictures: *cat, fan*

Circle the picture that <u>ends</u> with /**f**/.

_____f

Pictures: *leaf, pig*

Name _____

Listen for the Sound of Ff

Circle the pictures that <u>begin</u> with the same sound as **fish**.

Underline the pictures that <u>end</u> with the same sound as **calf**.

WEEK 2

Home–School Connection

To Parents

This week your child learned that **F** stands for the first sound in **fish** and the last sound in **calf**.

<u>f</u>ish | cal<u>f</u>

Pictures: *farm, leaf, fence, knife, elf, fan*

Trace and write the letters.

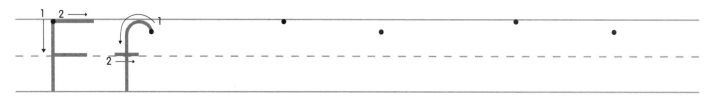

WEEK
3
Gg

Miss Goose and Miss Bug

Concept: G stands for the first sound in **goose** and the last sound in **bug**.
High-Frequency Words: I, like, the

Day 1

SKILLS:
Concepts of Print

• Identify uppercase and lowercase letters of the alphabet

Phonemic Awareness

• Recognize a phoneme in a spoken word

Phonics/Word Analysis

• Learn and apply letter-sound correspondences

• Produce the sound a consonant letter makes in isolation

Literary Response and Analysis

• Participate in a group response to a literary selection, identifying the characters, setting, and sequence of events

• Make predictions about text content using pictures, background knowledge, and text features

Comprehension

• Answer questions about text read aloud

• Respond to *who, what, where, why, how* questions about text read aloud

Learning About the Letter *Gg*

Distribute the Day 1 activity page. Say: *This week's letter is **G**. Find **G** at the top of the page. Point to the uppercase **G**. Now point to the lowercase **g**. Sometimes the letter **G** stands for this sound: /g/. Say /g/. (/g/) It is the first sound you hear in **goose**. Say **goose**. (goose) It is the <u>last</u> sound you hear in **bug**. Say **bug**. (bug) What sound does the letter **G** sometimes stand for? (/g/)*

Listening to the Story

To prepare students to listen to the story, say: *I am going to read you a story. The title is "Miss Goose and Miss Bug." Look at the picture. What do you think happens in the story? (students respond) Listen for the /g/ sound as I read the story.*

---

*One sunny afternoon, Miss **Goose** was taking a walk in Miss Bug's garden. She came upon a patch of **golden** sunflowers. "Hello, Miss Goose," buzzed Miss **Bug**. "Hello, Miss Bug. You have a lovely **garden**," honked Miss Goose. "Thank you. Please try a leaf." So Miss Bug and Miss Goose sat on a **twig** and munched on a leaf. When it was time for Miss Goose to **go**, she said, "Please join me for lunch tomorrow. The grass growing beside my **gate** is delicious." Miss Bug gave Miss Goose's **leg** a **hug** and said, "I'll see you tomorrow!"*

Thinking About the Story

Distribute crayons or markers. Guide students in answering questions about the story. Say:

Day 1 picture

• *Look at the big picture. Remember, the people or animals in a story are called the **characters**. Who are the characters in this story? (Miss Goose, Miss Bug) Make a yellow dot on Miss Goose. Make a red dot on Miss Bug.*

• *The place where a story happens is called the **setting**. Where does this story happen? (Miss Bug's garden) The setting is Miss Bug's garden.*

• *Look at the little pictures at the bottom of the page. Which picture shows what happened first? (Miss Goose going for a walk) Write **1** under the picture.*

• *Which picture shows what happened next? (Miss Goose and Miss Bug sharing a leaf) Write **2** under the picture.*

• *Which picture shows what happened at the end of the story? (Miss Bug giving Miss Goose's leg a hug) Write **3** under the picture.*

SKILLS:
Concepts of Print
- Locate a printed word on a page
- Follow words from top to bottom and left to right
- Track print by pointing to written words when text is read aloud by self or others

Phonemic Awareness
- Segment the initial phoneme of a spoken word

Phonics/Word Analysis
- Learn and apply letter-sound correspondences

Writing
- Print uppercase and lowercase letters
- Use spacing between letters and words when writing on a line

Reading and Writing Initial *G*

Distribute the Day 2 activity and a writing tool. Say:

- *Yesterday we read a story about a goose in a garden. Point to the goose at the top of the page. Say* **goose**. *(goose) What is the first sound in* **goose**? *(/g/) What letter stands for /g/? (G) Let's read the word* **goose** *together. Put your finger under the letter* **g**. *Move your finger under the word as you read it with me:* **goose**.

- *Now look at the pictures in the box. We're going to circle the pictures that begin with /g/. Point to the gorilla. Say* **gorilla**. *(gorilla) Does* **gorilla** *begin with /g/? (yes) Draw a circle around the gorilla.*

Repeat the process for the remaining pictures. Then direct students' attention to the next task. Say:

- *We are going to write uppercase* **G** *and lowercase* **g**. *Start at the black dot on uppercase* **G**. *Trace the line around. Go to the line below the number 2. Trace it across. Go to the next black dot. Write another uppercase* **G**.

Guide students through writing two more uppercase *G*s. Then say:

- *Now let's write lowercase* **g**. *Start at the black dot. Trace the line all the way around to make a circle. Go to the line next to the number 2. Follow the line down and then up. Now write three more lowercase* **g***'s.*

- *Look at the sentence at the bottom of the page. It says* **I like the goose**. *Move your finger under each word as you read it with me:* **I like the goose**. *Circle the word* **goose**.

Day 2 activity

SKILLS:
Concepts of Print
- Locate a printed word on a page
- Follow words from top to bottom and left to right
- Track print by pointing to written words when text is read aloud by self or others

Phonemic Awareness
- Segment the final phoneme of a spoken word

Phonics/Word Analysis
- Learn and apply letter-sound correspondences

Writing
- Print uppercase and lowercase letters
- Use spacing between letters and words when writing on a line

Reading and Writing Final *G*

Distribute the Day 3 activity and a writing tool. Say:

- *One of the characters in this week's story was named* **Miss Bug**. *Say* **bug**. *(bug) What is the last sound in* **bug**? *(/g/) What letter stands for /g/? (G) Let's read the word* **bug** *together. Put your finger under the letter* **b**. *Move your finger under the word as you read it with me:* **bug**.

- *Now look at the pictures in the box. We're going to circle the pictures that end with /g/. The first picture shows a leg. Point to the leg. Say* **leg**. *Does* **leg** *end with /g/? (yes) Draw a circle around the leg.*

Repeat the process for the remaining pictures. Then direct students' attention to the next task. Say:

- *Yesterday we followed the dots and the arrows to write uppercase and lowercase* **G***s. We are going to do it again today. Trace the uppercase* **G**. *Then start at each dot and write an uppercase* **G**.

- *Now trace the lowercase* **g**. *Then start at each dot and write a lowercase* **g**.

- *Look at the sentence at the bottom of the page. It says* **I like the bug**. *Move your finger under each word as you read it with me:* **I like the bug**. *Circle the word* **bug**.

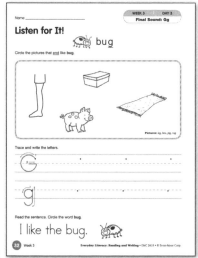

Day 3 activity

SKILLS:
Concepts of Print
- Locate a printed word on a page

Phonemic Awareness
- Identify the initial or final phoneme of a spoken word

Phonics/Word Recognition
- Recognize that individual letters have associated sounds

Literary Response and Analysis
- Participate in a group response to a literary selection, identifying the characters, setting, and sequence of events

Comprehension
- Answer questions about text read aloud
- Respond to *who, what, where, why, how* questions about text read aloud

Initial and Final *G*

Reread the Day 1 story. Then guide a discussion about the story by saying:

The setting of our story is Miss Bug's garden.

- *What did Miss Bug ask Miss Goose to try?* (a leaf)
- *What did Miss Goose invite Miss Bug to try?* (the grass by her gate)
- *What happened at the end of the story?* (Miss Bug gave Miss Goose's leg a hug.)

Then distribute the Day 4 activity and a writing tool. Say:

- *Point to the first sentence. Move your finger under each word as we read together: **I like the goose**. Let's read it again: **I like the goose**. Which picture belongs with this sentence?* (the goose) *Draw a line from the sentence to the goose.*
- *Point to the next sentence. Move your finger under each word as we read together: **I like the bug**. Let's read it again: **I like the bug**. Which picture belongs with this sentence?* (the bug) *Draw a line from the sentence to the bug.*
- *Now look at the first box at the bottom of the page. We are going to circle the picture that begins with **/g/**. Let's say each picture name together: **gate, mouse**. Which word begins with **/g/: gate** or **mouse**?* (gate) *Circle the gate. The word **gate** begins with the letter **g**.*
- *Now look at the next box. We are going to circle the picture that ends with **/g/**. Let's say each picture name together: **bee, rug**. Which word ends with **/g/: bee** or **rug**?* (rug) *Circle the rug. The word **rug** ends with the letter **g**.*

Day 4 activity

SKILLS:
Phonemic Awareness
- Identify the initial or final phoneme of a spoken word

Literary Response and Analysis
- Participate in a group response to a literary selection, identifying the characters, setting, and sequence of events

Comprehension
- Make connections using prior knowledge and real-life experiences

Circle Activity

Have students sit in a circle. Then review the Day 1 story and connect it to students' lives by asking:

- *Who were the characters in this week's story? Where were they?*
- *Does your family have a garden? What do you grow?*

Have students practice distinguishing the initial and final **G** sound using the call-and-response activity below. Begin by having students sit cross-legged. Then teach them to respond to your call by patting their left knee when they say "first" and their right knee when they say "last." If necessary, place a sticker on students' left knee to help them remember right from left.

Recite the chant below as you alternate patting knees and clapping as you say each syllable.

Teacher: *Lis-ten, lis-ten, do you hear it?*
*Let-ter **G**. Let-ter **G**.*
Is it first, or is it last?
*Tell me quick-ly, tell me fast: **goose**!*

Students: *First!* (pat left knee)

Teacher: ***Bug**!*

Students: *Last!* (pat right knee)

Repeat the chant using the following words: *golden, garden, gum, pig, leg, twig.*

Home–School Connection p. 34
Spanish version available (see p. 2)

Gg

Miss Goose and Miss Bug

Number the pictures in order.

Listen for It!

 <u>g</u>oose

Circle the pictures that begin like **goose**.

Pictures: *gorilla, gate, tree, girl*

Trace and write the letters.

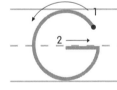

Read the sentence. Circle the word **goose**.

I like the goose.

Name _____

Listen for It!

 bu**g**

Circle the pictures that <u>end</u> like **bug**.

Pictures: *leg, box, pig, rug*

Trace and write the letters.

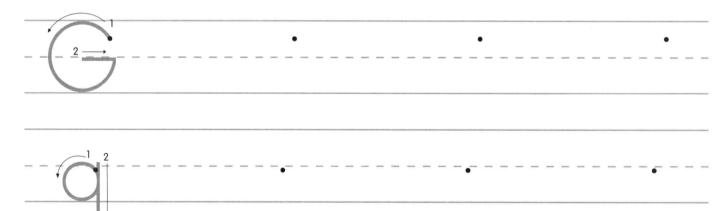

Read the sentence. Circle the word **bug**.

I like the bug.

Everyday Literacy: Reading and Writing • EMC 2418 • © Evan-Moor Corp.

Name _____

Read It!

Read the sentence.
Draw a line to the correct picture.

I like the goose.

I like the bug.

Circle the picture that begins with /g/.

Circle the picture that <u>ends</u> with /g/.

g____

____g

Pictures: *gate, mouse*

Pictures: *bee, rug*

Name _____

Listen for the Sound of Gg

Circle the pictures that <u>begin</u> with the same sound as **goose**.

Underline the pictures that <u>end</u> with the same sound as **bug**.

WEEK 3

Home–School Connection

To Parents

This week your child learned that **G** stands for the first sound in **goose** and the last sound in **bug**.

goose | bug

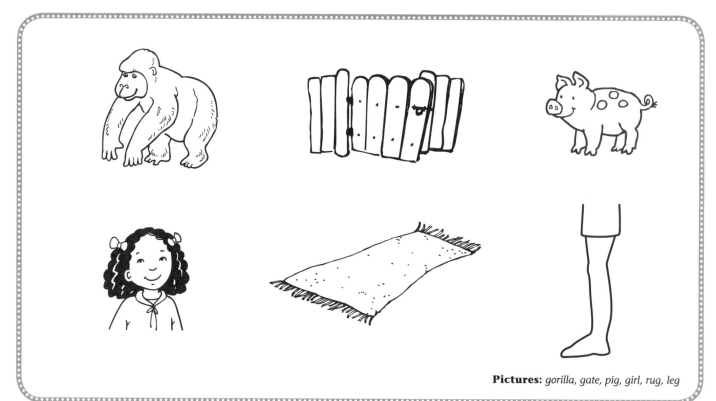

Pictures: *gorilla, gate, pig, girl, rug, leg*

Trace and write the letters.

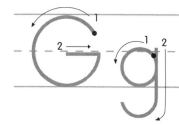

Everyday Literacy: Reading and Writing • EMC 2418 • © Evan-Moor Corp.

Concept

Initial and Final Sounds:

B, F, G

Review It

Vocabulary

Words with *b*, *f*, or *g* at the Beginning: bat, fairy, fire, gold, golden, goose

Words with *b*, *f*, or *g* at the End: cub, wolf, frog

High-Frequency Words: I, like, see, the

Day 1

SKILLS:
Concepts of Print
- Identify uppercase and lowercase letters of the alphabet

Phonemic Awareness
- Isolate and identify the initial or final phoneme of a spoken word

Phonics/Word Analysis
- Recognize that individual letters have associated sounds

Writing
- Print uppercase and lowercase letters
- Use spacing between letters and words when writing on a line

I Know *Bb*, *Ff*, and *Gg*

Distribute the Day 1 activity and a writing tool. Then say:

- *Point to the bat. What letter sound do you hear at the beginning of **bat**? (/b/) What letter stands for **/b/**? (B) Point to the uppercase **B**. Trace it. Now point to the lowercase **b**. Trace it. Now write two uppercase **B**s and two lowercase **b**'s on the line.*

- *Point to the fish. What letter sound do you hear at the beginning of **fish**? (/f/) What letter stands for **/f/**? (F) Point to the uppercase **F**. Trace it. Now point to the lowercase **f**. Trace it. Now write two uppercase **F**s and two lowercase **f**'s on the line.*

Day 1 activity

Repeat the process for the remaining picture and letters. Then direct students' attention to the next task. Say:

- *Look at the uppercase alphabet at the bottom of the page. Let's name the letters together. (name aloud) Circle uppercase **B**, **F**, and **G**.*

- *Look at the lowercase alphabet below. Let's name the letters together. (name aloud) Now circle lowercase **b**, **f**, and **g**.*

Day 2

SKILLS:
Phonemic Awareness
- Identify the position of an isolated phoneme in a spoken word

Phonics/Word Analysis
- Learn and apply letter-sound correspondences
- Recognize that individual letters have associated sounds
- Read familiar CVC words and common sight words

Listening for *Bb*, *Ff*, and *Gg*

Distribute the Day 2 activity and a writing tool to each student. Say:

- *We are going to listen for letter sounds. Point to the **B** row. What sound does **B** stand for? (/b/) Say **book**. (book) Do you hear **/b/** first or last in **book**? (first) Fill in the first circle under the book. Say **tub**. (tub) Do you hear **/b/** first or last in **tub**? (last) Fill in the last circle. Say **ball**. (ball) Do you hear **/b/** first or last in **ball**? (first) Fill in the first circle under the ball.*

- *Point to the **F** row. What sound does **F** stand for? (/f/) Say **fence**. (fence) Do you hear **/f/** first or last in **fence**? (first) Fill in the first circle under the fence. Say **flower**. Do you hear **/f/** first or last in **flower**? (first) Fill in the first circle under the flower. Say **calf**. Do you hear **/f/** first or last in **calf**? (last) Fill in the last circle under the calf.*

Day 2 activity

Repeat the process for the remaining letter and pictures. Then direct students' attention to the next task. Say:

- *Point to the sentence at the bottom of the page. Move your finger under each word as you read it aloud. Now fill in the circle beside the matching picture.*

SKILLS:
Concepts of Print
• Understand that spoken words are represented in writing by specific sequences of letters

Phonemic Awareness
• Isolate and identify the initial or final sound of a spoken word

Phonics/Word Analysis
• Learn and apply letter-sound correspondences
• Recognize that individual letters have associated sounds
• Read familiar CVC words and common sight words

Writing
• Write the letters that match sounds in words

Writing Words with *B, F,* and *G*

Distribute the Day 3 activity and a writing tool to each student. Say:

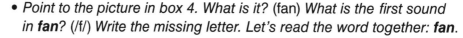

• *Each box shows a picture and a word that is missing a letter. We are going to say each picture name and write the missing letter. Point to the first picture. What is it?* (bag) *What is the first sound in* **bag**? (/b/) *Write the missing letter. Now move your finger under each letter as we read the word together:* **bag**.

• *Point to the picture in box 2. What is it?* (gum) *What is the first sound in* **gum**? (/g/) *Write the missing letter. Let's read the word together:* **gum**.

• *Point to the picture in box 3. What is it?* (pig) *What is the* last *sound in* **pig**? (/g/) *Write the missing letter. Let's read the word together:* **pig**.

• *Point to the picture in box 4. What is it?* (fan) *What is the first sound in* **fan**? (/f/) *Write the missing letter. Let's read the word together:* **fan**.

• *Point to the picture in box 5. What is it?* (elf) *What is the* last *sound in* **elf**? (/f/) *Write the missing letter. Let's read the word together:* **elf**.

• *Point to the picture in box 6. What is it?* (web) *What is the* last *sound in* **web**? (/b/) *Write the missing letter. Let's read the word together:* **web**.

Day 3 activity

SKILLS:
Phonics/Word Analysis
• Learn and apply letter-sound correspondences
• Read familiar CVC words and common sight words

Comprehension
• Demonstrate comprehension of text read aloud by self or others

Reading Words with *B, F,* and *G*

Distribute the Day 4 activity and pencils or crayons. Say:

• *Point to the first sentence. Move your finger under the words as we read together:* **I see the bat**. *Draw a line from this sentence to the picture it matches.*

• *Point to sentence 2. Move your finger under the words as we read together:* **I see the cub**. *Draw a line from the sentence to the picture it matches.*

• *Point to sentence 3. Let's read it together:* **I see the fish**. *Draw a line from the sentence to the picture it matches.*

• *Point to sentence 4. Let's read it together:* **I see the calf**. *Draw a line from the sentence to the picture it matches.*

• *Point to sentence 5. Let's read it together:* **I see the goose**. *Draw a line from the sentence to the picture it matches.*

• *Point to sentence 6. Let's read it together:* **I see the pig**. *Draw a line from the sentence to the picture it matches.*

SKILLS:

Phonemic Awareness

• Isolate and identify the initial or final phoneme of a spoken word

Phonics/Word Analysis

• Learn and apply letter-sound correspondences

• Recognize that individual letters have associated sounds

Home–School Connection p. 42
Spanish version available (see p. 2)

Phonics Review Game

Play the following game to review the initial and final consonant sounds that students have learned this week.

Materials: 6 large index cards or 3 sheets of construction paper cut in half

Preparation: Write the letter **b** on two cards, the letter **f** on two cards, and the letter **g** on two cards. Divide the cards into two sets that contain one of each letter. Display one set of cards on each end of the board.

How to Play: Divide students into two teams. Have each team line up facing the board. Explain to students that you will say a word and that they should listen for the beginning sound. After you say the word, the first player in each line races up to the board, chooses the correct letter card, faces his or her team, and says the letter name aloud. Each correct answer is worth one point. The two players then return the cards to the ledge and go to the end of the line. Repeat the process until you have called all of the words in the chart below. The team with the most points wins. Play the game again, and have students listen for ending sounds.

Beginning Sounds:	**Ending Sounds:**
B: bat, bear, big, book, ball	**B:** cub, job, cab, tub, tab
F: fairy, fun, fire, feather, fox	**F:** wolf, huff, puff, leaf, elf
G: goose, gold, good, goat, gas	**G:** bag, frog, log, bug, dog

Write It!

Trace then write each letter.

 Bb ----------

 Ff ----------

 Gg ----------

Find uppercase **B**, **F**, and **G**. Circle them.

A	B	C	D	E	F	G	H	I	J	K	L	M
N	O	P	Q	R	S	T	U	V	W	X	Y	Z

Find lowercase **b**, **f**, and **g**. Circle them.

a	b	c	d	e	f	g	h	i	j	k	l	m
n	o	p	q	r	s	t	u	v	w	x	y	z

Name _____

Listen for It!

Where do you hear the letter sound?
Fill in the circle to show **first** or **last**.

Bb

○——○   ○——○   ○——○

Ff

○——○   ○——○   ○——○

Gg

○——○   ○——○   ○——○

Read the sentence.
Fill in the circle next to the correct picture.

○

I like the fish.

○

Name _____

Spell It!

Say each picture name.
Write the missing letter.

b f g

1

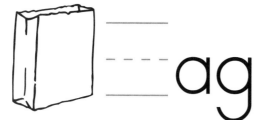 __ ag

2

__ um

3

 pi __

4

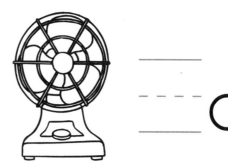 __ an

5

 el __

6

 we __

Name _____

Read It!

Read the sentence.
Draw a line to the correct picture.

1 I see the bat.

2 I see the cub.

3 I see the fish.

4 I see the calf.

5 I see the goose.

6 I see the pig.

Name _____

Beginning and Ending
Bb Ff Gg

WEEK 4

Home–School Connection

To Parents

This week your child reviewed beginning and ending sounds for the letters **B**, **F**, and **G**.

Name each picture. Draw a line to show what letter sound you hear at the **beginning**.

g

b

f

Pictures: *flag, ball, gum*

Name each picture. Draw a line to show what letter sound you hear at the **end**.

f

b

g

Pictures: *leg, leaf, web*

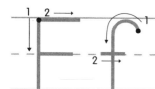

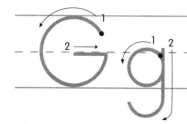

Everyday Literacy: Reading and Writing • EMC 2418 • © Evan-Moor Corp.

WEEK 5
Ss

Octopus in the Sea

Concept: S stands for the first sound in **seal** and the last sound in **octopus**.
High-Frequency Words: *a, an, here, is*

SKILLS:

Concepts of Print
• Identify uppercase and lowercase letters of the alphabet

Phonemic Awareness
• Recognize a phoneme in a spoken word

Phonics/Word Analysis
• Learn and apply letter-sound correspondences
• Produce the sound a consonant letter makes in isolation

Literary Response and Analysis
• Participate in a group response to a literary selection, identifying the characters, setting, and sequence of events
• Make predictions about text content using pictures, background knowledge, and text features

Comprehension
• Answer questions about text read aloud
• Respond to *who, what, where, why, how* questions about text read aloud

Learning About the Letter *Ss*

Distribute the Day 1 activity page. Say: *This week's letter is* **S**. *Find* **S** *at the top of the page. Point to the uppercase* **S**. *Now point to the lowercase* **s**. *The letter* **S** *stands for this sound:* **/s/**. *Say* **/s/**. *(/s/) It is the first sound you hear in* **seal**. *Say* **seal**. *(seal) It is the* last *sound you hear in* **octopus**. *Say* **octopus**. *(octopus) What sound does the letter* **S** *stand for? (/s/)*

Listening to the Story

To prepare students to listen to the story, say: *I am going to read you a story. The title is "Octopus in the Sea." Look at the picture. What do you think happens in the story? (students respond) Listen for the /s/ sound as I read the story.*

I am an **octopus**. *I live in the* **sea**. *The sea has a lot of animals in it. Sometimes it can be scary, but I have figured out what to do to take care of myself. When I see a* **seal** *or another animal that wants to eat me, I zoom away and hide in the tall sea* **grass**. *Another thing I do is change color. I make myself the same color as* **sand** *or* **rocks**, *so it's hard for animals to see me. And if a really scary ocean animal comes looking for me, I* **surprise** *it with a squirt of my ink and use my eight arms to swim away. An octopus has to be smart to* **survive** *in the sea!*

Thinking About the Story

Distribute crayons or markers. Guide students in answering questions about the story. Say:

• *What is the title of the story? (Octopus in the Sea) Do you hear /s/ in* **sea**? *(yes) Look at the big picture. Make a blue dot on the water.*

• *There are two big animals and many small animals in this picture. Name the big animals. (octopus and seal) Do you hear /s/ in* **octopus**? *(yes) Make a red dot on the octopus. Do you hear /s/ in* **seal**? *(yes) Make a black dot on the seal.*

• *Now look at the little pictures at the bottom of the page. The octopus figured out three things to do to take care of itself. Which picture shows the first thing? (octopus swimming away and hiding in sea grass) Write* **1** *under the picture.*

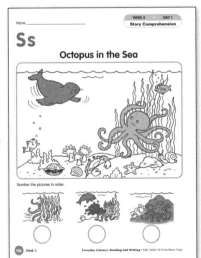

Day 1 picture

• *Which picture shows the next thing? (octopus changing color) Write* **2** *under it.*

• *What is the last thing the octopus does to take care of itself? (squirting ink and using arms to swim away) Write* **3** *under the picture.*

SKILLS:

Concepts of Print

- Locate a printed word on a page
- Follow words from top to bottom and left to right
- Track print by pointing to written words when text is read aloud by self or others

Phonemic Awareness

- Segment the initial phoneme of a spoken word

Phonics/Word Analysis

- Learn and apply letter-sound correspondences

Writing

- Print uppercase and lowercase letters
- Use spacing between letters and words when writing on a line

Reading and Writing Initial *S*

Distribute the Day 2 activity and a writing tool. Say:

- *Yesterday we read a story about an octopus who protects itself from seals. Point to the seal at the top of the page. Say* **seal**. *(seal) What is the first sound in* **seal**? *(/s/) What letter stands for /s/? (S) Let's read the word* **seal** *together. Put your finger under the letter* **s**. *Move your finger under the word as you read it with me:* **seal**.

- *Now look at the pictures in the box. We're going to circle the pictures that* begin *with /s/. Point to the soap. Say* **soap**. *(soap)* Does **soap** begin with /s/? *(yes) Draw a circle around the soap.*

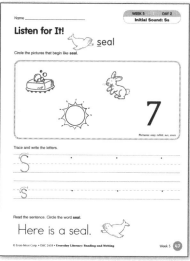

Day 2 activity

Repeat the process for the remaining pictures. Then direct students' attention to the next task. Say:

- *We are going to write uppercase* **S** *and lowercase* **s**. *Start at the black dot on uppercase* **S**. *Trace the line around the first curve and around the second curve. Go to the next black dot. Write another uppercase* **S**.

Guide students through writing two more uppercase Ss. Then say:

- *Now let's write lowercase* **s**. *Start at the black dot. Trace the line around the first curve and around the second curve. Now write three more lowercase* **s***'s.*

- *Look at the sentence at the bottom of the page. It says* **Here is a seal**. *Move your finger under each word as you read it with me:* **Here is a seal**. *Circle the word* **seal**.

SKILLS:

Concepts of Print

- Locate a printed word on a page
- Follow words from top to bottom and left to right
- Track print by pointing to written words when text is read aloud by self or others

Phonemic Awareness

- Segment the final phoneme of a spoken word

Phonics/Word Analysis

- Learn and apply letter-sound correspondences

Writing

- Print uppercase and lowercase letters
- Use spacing between letters and words when writing on a line

Reading and Writing Final *S*

Distribute the Day 3 activity and a writing tool. Say:

- *The octopus in the story figured out things to do to take care of itself. Point to the octopus at the top of the page. Say* **octopus**. *(octopus) What is the* last *sound in* **octopus**? *(/s/) What letter stands for /s/? (S) Let's read the word* **octopus** *together. Put your finger under the letter* **o**. *Move your finger under the word as you read it with me:* **octopus**.

- *Now look at the pictures in the box. We're going to circle the pictures that* end *with /s/. Put your finger on the lips. Say* **lips**. *(lips) Does* **lips** *end with /s/? (yes) Draw a circle around the lips.*

Day 3 activity

Repeat the process for the remaining pictures. Then direct students' attention to the next task. Say:

- *Yesterday we followed the dots and the arrows to write uppercase and lowercase* **S***s. We are going to do it again today. Trace the uppercase* **S**. *Then start at each dot and write an uppercase* **S**.

- *Now trace the lowercase* **s**. *Then start at each dot and write a lowercase* **s**.

- *Look at the sentence at the bottom of the page. It says* **Here is an octopus**. *Move your finger under each word as you read it with me:* **Here is an octopus**. *Circle the word* **octopus**.

Everyday Literacy: Reading and Writing • EMC 2418 • © Evan-Moor Corp.

Initial and Final S

Reread the Day 1 story. Then guide a discussion about the story by saying:

The title of the story is "Octopus in the Sea."

• *Where does the octopus live?* (in the sea)

• *Where did the octopus hide?* (in the sea grass)

• *How does the octopus surprise scary ocean animals?* (squirts them with ink)

Then distribute the Day 4 activity and a writing tool. Say:

Day 4 activity

• *Point to the first sentence. Move your finger under each word as we read together:* **Here is a seal.** *Let's read it again:* **Here is a seal.** *Which picture belongs with this sentence?* (the seal) *Draw a line from the sentence to the seal.*

• *Point to the next sentence. Move your finger under each word as we read together:* **Here is an octopus.** *Let's read it again:* **Here is an octopus.** *Which picture belongs with this sentence?* (the octopus) *Draw a line from the sentence to the octopus.*

• *Now look at the first box at the bottom of the page. We are listening for the word that begins with /s/. Let's name the pictures together:* **cake, sun.** *Which word begins with /s/:* **cake** *or* **sun***?* (sun) *Circle the sun. The word* **sun** *begins with the letter* **s.**

• *Now look at the next box. We are going to circle the picture that ends with /s/. Let's say each picture name together:* **lips, apple.** *Which word ends with /s/:* **lips** *or* **apple***?* (lips) *Circle the lips. The word* **lips** *ends with the letter* **s.**

Circle Activity

Have students sit in a circle. Then review the Day 1 story and connect it to students' lives by asking:

• *What does the title tell you about the story?*

• *Why does the octopus change color?*

• *Have you ever seen a real octopus? What did it look like?*

Have students practice distinguishing the initial and final **S** sound using the call-and-response activity below. Begin by having students sit cross-legged. Then teach them to respond to your call by patting their left knee when they say "first" and their right knee when they say "last." If necessary, place a sticker on students' left knee to help them remember right from left.

Recite the chant below as you alternate patting knees and clapping as you say each syllable.

Teacher: *Lis-ten, lis-ten, do you hear it?*
Let-ter **S***. Let-ter* **S***.*
Is it first, or is it last?
Tell me quick-ly, tell me fast: **seal***!*

Students: *First!* (pat left knee)

Teacher: *Octopus!*

Students: *Last!* (pat right knee)

Repeat the chant using the following words: *sand, sun, soap, dress, grass, rocks.*

Name _____

Ss

Octopus in the Sea

Number the pictures in order.

◯ ◯ ◯

Listen for It!

 <u>s</u>eal

Circle the pictures that begin like **seal**.

Pictures: *soap, rabbit, sun, seven*

Trace and write the letters.

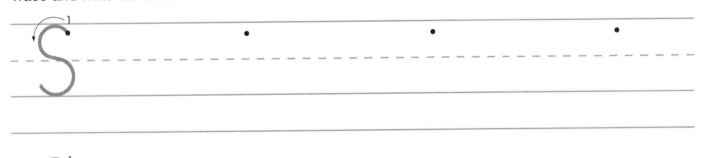

Read the sentence. Circle the word **seal**.

Here is a seal.

Listen for It!

 octopu<u>s</u>

Circle the pictures that <u>end</u> like **octopus**.

Pictures: *lips, grass, owl, dress*

Trace and write the letters.

Read the sentence. Circle the word **octopus**.

Here is an octopus.

Name _____

Read It!

Read the sentence.
Draw a line to the correct picture.

Here is a seal.

★

Here is an octopus.

★

Circle the picture that begins with /s/.

Circle the picture that ends with /s/.

S____

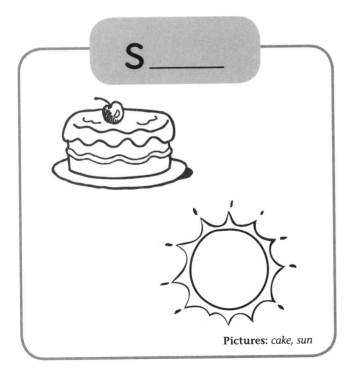

Pictures: *cake, sun*

____S

Pictures: *lips, apple*

Name _____

Listen for the Sound of S̲s̲

Circle the pictures that <u>begin</u> with the same sound as **seal**.

Underline the pictures that <u>end</u> with the same sound as **octopus**.

s̲eal   octopu̲s̲

Pictures: *sun, dress, soap, grass, lips, seven*

Trace and write the letters.

Cool, Dark Night

Concept: **L** stands for the first sound in **lion** and the last sound in **cool**.
High-Frequency Words: a, an, is, this

SKILLS:

Concepts of Print
• Identify uppercase and lowercase letters of the alphabet

Phonemic Awareness
• Recognize a phoneme in a spoken word

Phonics/Word Analysis
• Learn and apply letter-sound correspondences
• Produce the sound a consonant letter makes in isolation

Literary Response and Analysis
• Participate in a group response to a literary selection, identifying the characters, setting, and sequence of events
• Make predictions about text content using pictures, background knowledge, and text features

Comprehension
• Answer questions about text read aloud
• Respond to who, what, where, why, how questions about text read aloud

Learning About the Letter *Ll*

Distribute the Day 1 activity page. Say: *This week's letter is **L**. Find **L** at the top of the page. Point to the uppercase **L**. Now point to the lowercase **l**. The letter **L** stands for this sound: /l/. Say /l/. (/l/) It is the first sound you hear in **lion**. Say **lion**. (lion) It is the last sound you hear in **owl**. Say **owl**. (owl) What sound does the letter **L** stand for? (/l/)*

Listening to the Story

To prepare students to listen to the story, say: *I am going to read you a story called "Cool, Dark Night." Look at the picture. What do you think happens in the story? (students respond) Listen for the /l/ sound as I read the story.*

---

*It was a **cool**, dark night. The moon was hanging in the sky above the **hill**. It was quiet inside our tent. "It's **late**," said Jason. "I bet we're the only ones awake." Suddenly, we heard a noise. "What was that?" I asked. "I don't know," said Jason. "Maybe it's a **lion**. Lions hunt at night." I turned on my **light** to look outside. We poked our heads outside the tent and **listened**. We didn't hear anything, but we saw something move in the tree. I shined my **light** on it. "**Look**, it's not a **lion**. It's an **owl** sitting in the tree. I guess we're not the only ones awake after **all**."*

Thinking About the Story

Distribute crayons or markers. Guide students in answering questions about the story. Say:

• *Look at the big picture. Who are the characters in the story? (Jason and another boy)*

• *Remember, the place where the story happens is called the **setting**. What is the setting of this story? (outdoors; a tent) What did the boys think might be outside the tent? (a lion) Do you hear /l/ in **lion**? (yes)*

• *Look at the little pictures at the bottom of the page. Which picture shows what happened first in the story? (boys heard noise and turned on light) Write **1** under the picture.*

• *What happened next? (boys looked outside) Write **2** under the picture.*

• *What did the boys do last? (shined light onto owl in tree) Write **3** under the picture.*

Day 1 picture

SKILLS:
Concepts of Print
- Locate a printed word on a page
- Follow words from top to bottom and left to right
- Track print by pointing to written words when text is read aloud by self or others

Phonemic Awareness
- Segment the initial phoneme of a spoken word

Phonics/Word Analysis
- Learn and apply letter-sound correspondences

Writing
- Print uppercase and lowercase letters
- Use spacing between letters and words when writing on a line

Reading and Writing Initial *L*

Distribute the Day 2 activity and a writing tool. Say:

- *Yesterday we read a story about two boys who thought there might be a lion outside their tent. Point to the lion at the top of the page. Say **lion**. (lion) What is the first sound in **lion**? (/l/) What letter stands for /l/? (L) Let's read the word **lion** together. Put your finger under the letter l. Move your finger under the word as you read it with me: **lion**.*

- *Now look at the pictures in the box. We're going to circle the pictures that begin with /l/. Point to the lamp. Say **lamp**. (lamp) Does **lamp** begin with /l/? (yes) Draw a circle around the lamp.*

Repeat the process for the remaining pictures. Then direct students' attention to the next task. Say:

Day 2 activity

- *We are going to write uppercase **L** and lowercase **l**. Start at the black dot on uppercase **L**. Trace the line down and across. Go to the next black dot. Write another uppercase **L**.*

Guide students through writing two more uppercase Ls. Then say:

- *Now let's write lowercase **l**. Start at the black dot. Trace the line down. Now write three more lowercase **l**'s.*

- *Look at the sentence at the bottom of the page. It says **This is a lion**. Move your finger under each word as you read it with me: **This is a lion**. Circle the word **lion**.*

SKILLS:
Concepts of Print
- Locate a printed word on a page
- Follow words from top to bottom and left to right
- Track print by pointing to written words when text is read aloud by self or others

Phonemic Awareness
- Segment the final phoneme of a spoken word

Phonics/Word Analysis
- Learn and apply letter-sound correspondences

Writing
- Print uppercase and lowercase letters
- Use spacing between letters and words when writing on a line

Reading and Writing Final *L*

Distribute the Day 3 activity and a writing tool. Say:

- *The boys in our story saw an owl in a tree. Point to the owl at the top of the page. Say **owl**. (owl) What is the last sound in **owl**? (/l/) What letter stands for /l/? (L) Let's read the word **owl** together. Put your finger under the letter o. Move your finger under the word as you read it with me: **owl**.*

- *Now look at the pictures in the box. We're going to circle the pictures that end with /l/. Put your finger on the ball. Say **ball**. (ball) Does **ball** end with /l/? (yes) Draw a circle around the ball.*

Repeat the process for the remaining pictures. Then direct students' attention to the next task. Say:

Day 3 activity

- *Yesterday we followed the dots and the arrows to write uppercase and lowercase Ls. We are going to do it again today. Trace the uppercase **L**. Then start at each dot and write an uppercase **L**.*

- *Now trace the lowercase **l**. Then start at each dot and write a lowercase **l**.*

- *Look at the sentence at the bottom of the page. It says **This is an owl**. Move your finger under each word as you read it with me: **This is an owl**. Circle the word **owl**.*

Initial and Final *L*

Reread the Day 1 story. Then guide a discussion about the story by saying:

We read about boys who were awake late at night.

• *Where were the boys?* (in a tent; outside)

• *Why did the boys look outside the tent?* (They heard a noise.)

• *What animal did they think they might see?* (a lion)

• *What animal did they see?* (an owl)

Then distribute the Day 4 activity and a writing tool. Say:

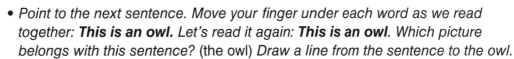

Day 4 activity

• *Point to the first sentence. Move your finger under each word as we read together:* **This is a lion.** *Let's read it again:* **This is a lion.** *Which picture belongs with this sentence?* (the lion) *Draw a line from the sentence to the lion.*

• *Point to the next sentence. Move your finger under each word as we read together:* **This is an owl.** *Let's read it again:* **This is an owl.** *Which picture belongs with this sentence?* (the owl) *Draw a line from the sentence to the owl.*

• *Now look at the first box at the bottom of the page. We are listening for the word that <u>begins</u> with /l/. Let's name the pictures together:* **log, tree.** *Which word begins with /l/:* **log** *or* **tree**? (log) *Circle the log. The word* **log** *begins with the letter* **l**.

• *Now look at the next box. We are going to circle the picture that <u>ends</u> with /l/. Let's say each picture name together:* **elf, towel.** *Which word ends with /l/:* **elf** *or* **towel**? (towel) *Circle the towel. The word* **towel** *ends with the letter* **l**.

Circle Activity

Have students sit in a circle. Then review the Day 1 story and connect it to students' lives by asking:

• *Have you ever heard a strange sound at night?*

• *Have you ever slept in a tent?*

Have students practice distinguishing the initial and final **L** sound using the call-and-response activity below. Begin by having students sit cross-legged. Then teach them to respond to your call by patting their left knee when they say "first" and their right knee when they say "last." If necessary, place a sticker on students' left knee to help them remember right from left.

Recite the chant below as you alternate patting knees and clapping as you say each syllable.

Teacher: *Lis-ten, lis-ten, do you hear it?*
Let-ter **L**. *Let-ter* **L**.
Is it first, or is it last?
Tell me quick-ly, tell me fast: **lion**!

Students: *First!* (pat left knee)

Teacher: *Owl!*

Students: *Last!* (pat right knee)

Repeat the chant using the following words: *light, leaf, lamp, nail, hill, cool.*

Ll

Cool, Dark Night

Number the pictures in order.

Name _____

Listen for It!

 <u>l</u>ion

Circle the pictures that begin like **lion**.

Pictures: *lamp, leaf, book, log*

Trace and write the letters.

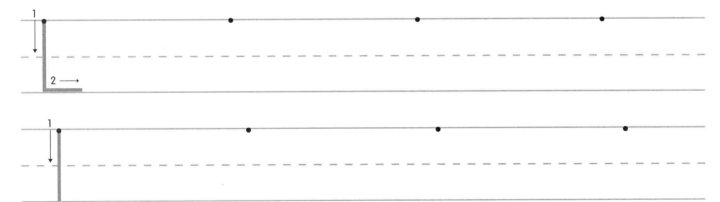

Read the sentence. Circle the word **lion**.

This is a lion.

Name _____

Listen for It!

 ow**l**

Circle the pictures that <u>end</u> like **owl**.

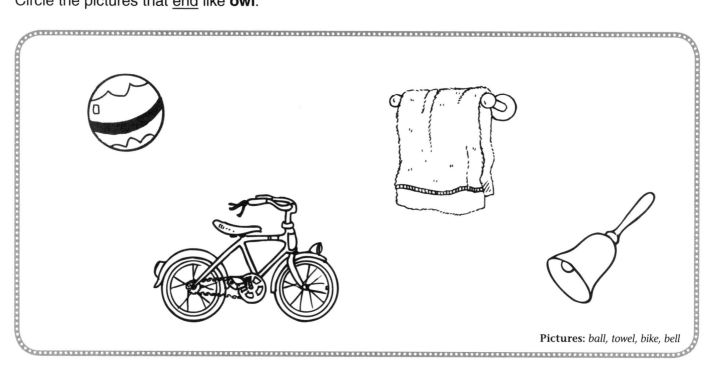

Pictures: *ball, towel, bike, bell*

Trace and write the letters.

Read the sentence. Circle the word **owl**.

This is an owl.

Name _____

Read It!

Read the sentence.
Draw a line to the correct picture.

This is a lion.   ★

This is an owl.   ★

Circle the picture that begins with /l/.

| l _____ |
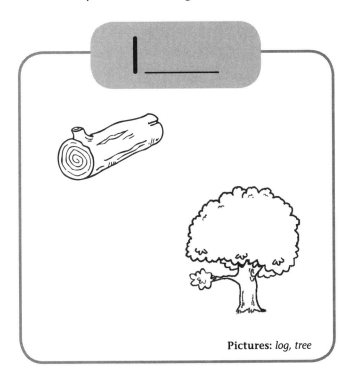
Pictures: *log, tree*

Circle the picture that ends with /l/.

| _____ l |
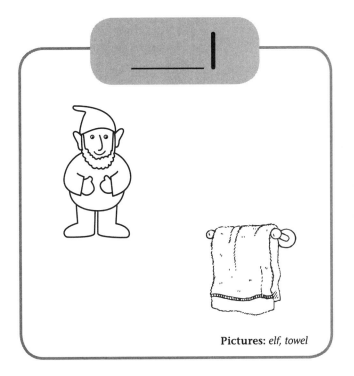
Pictures: *elf, towel*

Name _____

Listen for the Sound of Ll

Circle the pictures that <u>begin</u> with the same sound as **lion**.

Underline the pictures that <u>end</u> with the same sound as **owl**.

WEEK 6

Home–School Connection

To Parents

This week your child learned that **L** stands for the first sound in **lion** and the last sound in **owl**.

<u>l</u>ion | ow<u>l</u>

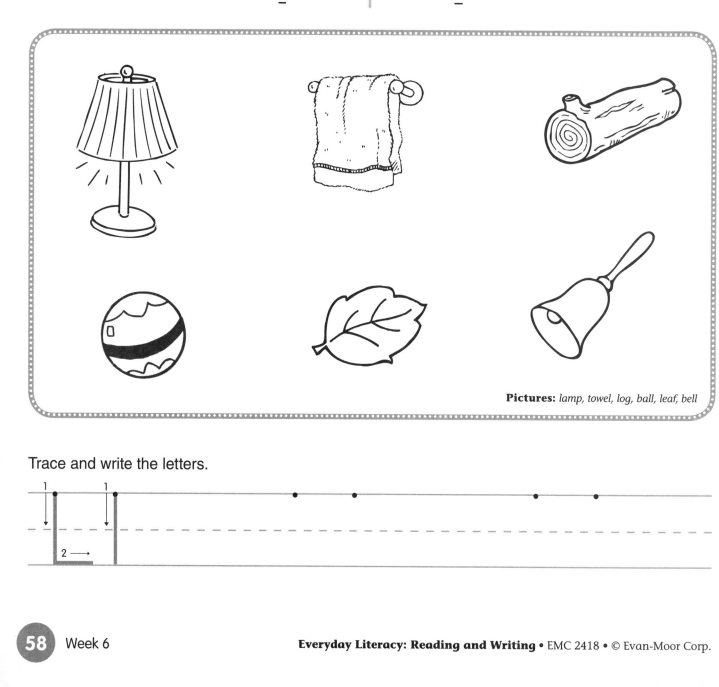

Pictures: *lamp, towel, log, ball, leaf, bell*

Trace and write the letters.

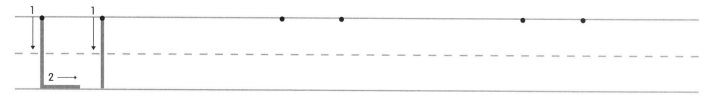

Everyday Literacy: Reading and Writing • EMC 2418 • © Evan-Moor Corp.

Digging for Clams

Concept: **M** stands for the first sound in **mouse** and the last sound in **clam**.

High-Frequency Words: *a, is, small, this*

Day 1

SKILLS:

Concepts of Print

• Identify uppercase and lowercase letters of the alphabet

Phonemic Awareness

• Recognize a phoneme in a spoken word

Phonics/Word Analysis

• Learn and apply letter-sound correspondences

• Produce the sound a consonant letter makes in isolation

Literary Response and Analysis

• Participate in a group response to a literary selection, identifying the characters, setting, and sequence of events

• Make predictions about text content using pictures, background knowledge, and text features

Comprehension

• Answer questions about text read aloud

• Respond to *who, what, where, why, how* questions about text read aloud

Learning About the Letter *Mm*

Distribute the Day 1 activity page. Say: *This week's letter is* **M**. *Find* **M** *at the top of the page. Point to the uppercase* **M**. *Now point to the lowercase* **m**. *The letter* **M** *stands for this sound: /m/. Say /m/. (/m/) It is the first sound you hear in* **mouse**. *Say* **mouse**. *(mouse) It is the* last *sound you hear in* **clam**. *Say* **clam**. *(clam) What sound does the letter* **M** *stand for? (/m/)*

Listening to the Story

To prepare students to listen to the story, say: *I am going to read you a story. The title is "Digging for Clams." Look at the picture. What do you think happens in the story? (students respond) Listen for the* **/m/** *sound as I read the story.*

Once a week, **my** *pet* **mouse Sam** *and I visit Grandpa. We do fun things together. Last week we went to the beach to dig up clams. Clams* **make** *little holes in the* **mud**. *Grandpa says if you find a little hole, there's probably a* **clam** *in it. I helped him look for holes. Every time we found a hole, we used our shovel to dig out a clam. We put the cold, sandy clams in our bucket. After we'd found enough clams, it was time to go home. Grandpa cooked clam chowder for dinner.* **Yum***!*

Thinking About the Story

Distribute crayons or markers. Guide students in answering questions about the story. Say:

Day 1 picture

• *What is the setting of this story? (the beach)*

• *Look at the big picture. What kind of animal does the boy have in his pocket? (a mouse) Do you hear* **/m/** *in* **mouse***? (yes) What is the mouse's name? (Sam) Do you hear* **/m/** *in* **Sam***? (yes) Make a red dot on Sam the mouse.*

• *What were Sam, the boy, and his grandpa doing at the beach? (digging up clams) Circle a clam.*

• *Do you think the boy likes clam chowder? Tell why. (Yes. He says "Yum!")*

• *Look at the little pictures at the bottom of the page. Which picture shows what happened first in the story? (boy looking for holes in the mud) Write* **1** *under the picture.*

• *What happened next? (digging up clams) Write* **2** *under the picture.*

• *What happened last? (eating clam chowder) Write* **3** *under the picture.*

SKILLS:

Concepts of Print

- Locate a printed word on a page
- Follow words from top to bottom and left to right
- Track print by pointing to written words when text is read aloud by self or others

Phonemic Awareness

- Segment the initial phoneme of a spoken word

Phonics/Word Analysis

- Learn and apply letter-sound correspondences

Writing

- Print uppercase and lowercase letters
- Use spacing between letters and words when writing on a line

Reading and Writing Initial *M*

Distribute the Day 2 activity and a writing tool. Say:

- *Yesterday we read a story about a boy who has a pet mouse. Point to the mouse at the top of the page. Say **mouse**. (mouse) What is the first sound in **mouse**? (/m/) What letter stands for /m/? (M) Let's read the word **mouse** together. Move your finger under the word as you read it with me: **mouse**.*

- *Now look at the pictures in the box. We're going to circle the pictures that <u>begin</u> with /m/. Point to the moon. Say **moon**. (moon) Does **moon** begin with /m/? (yes) Draw a circle around the moon.*

Repeat the process for the remaining pictures. Then direct students' attention to the next task. Say:

Day 2 activity

- *We are going to write uppercase **M** and lowercase **m**. Start at the black dot on uppercase **M**. Trace the line down. Go to the black dot again. Trace the line down and up to the number 2 and down again. Go to the next black dot. Write another uppercase **M**.*

Guide students through writing two more uppercase **M**s. Then say:

- *Now let's write lowercase **m**. Start at the black dot. Trace the line down. Go to the black dot again and trace over and down and up and over and down again. Now write three more lowercase **m**'s.*

- *Look at the sentence at the bottom of the page. It says **This is a small mouse**. Move your finger under each word as you read it with me: **This is a small mouse**. Circle the word **mouse**.*

SKILLS:

Concepts of Print

- Locate a printed word on a page
- Follow words from top to bottom and left to right
- Track print by pointing to written words when text is read aloud by self or others

Phonemic Awareness

- Segment the final phoneme of a spoken word

Phonics/Word Analysis

- Learn and apply letter-sound correspondences

Writing

- Print uppercase and lowercase letters
- Use spacing between letters and words when writing on a line

Reading and Writing Final *M*

Distribute the Day 3 activity and a writing tool. Say:

- *The boy in our story was digging for clams. Point to the clam. Say **clam**. (clam) What is the <u>last</u> sound in **clam**? (/m/) What letter stands for /m/? (M) Let's read the word **clam** together. Put your finger under the letter **c**. Move your finger under the word as you read it with me: **clam**.*

- *Now look at the pictures in the box. We're going to circle the pictures that <u>end</u> with /m/. Put your finger on the worm. Say **worm**. (worm) Does **worm** end with /m/? (yes) Circle the worm.*

Repeat the process for the remaining pictures. Then direct students' attention to the next task. Say:

Day 3 activity

- *Yesterday we followed the dots and the arrows to write uppercase and lowercase **M**s. We are going to do it again today. Trace the uppercase **M**. Then start at each dot and write an uppercase **M**.*

- *Now trace the lowercase **m**. Then start at each dot and write a lowercase **m**.*

- *Look at the sentence at the bottom of the page. It says **This is a small clam**. Move your finger under each word as you read it with me: **This is a small clam**. Circle the word **clam**.*

SKILLS:
Concepts of Print
• Locate a printed word on a page

Phonemic Awareness
• Identify the initial or final phoneme of a spoken word

Phonics/Word Recognition
• Recognize that individual letters have associated sounds

Literary Response and Analysis
• Participate in a group response to a literary selection, identifying the characters, setting, and sequence of events

Comprehension
• Answer questions about text read aloud
• Respond to *who, what, where, why, how* questions about text read aloud

Initial and Final *M*

Reread the Day 1 story. Then guide a discussion about the story by saying:

The title of our story this week is "Digging for Clams."

- *Who went digging for clams?* (grandpa, boy, and Sam the mouse)

- *What did they do with the clams?* (put them in a bucket; made clam chowder)

- *How did they know where to find the clams?* (looked for little holes in the mud/sand)

Then distribute the Day 4 activity and a writing tool. Say:

- *Point to the first sentence. Move your finger under each word as we read together:* **This is a small mouse.** *Let's read it again:* **This is a small mouse.** *Which picture belongs with this sentence?* (the mouse) *Draw a line to the mouse.*

- *Point to the next sentence. Move your finger under each word as we read together:* **This is a small clam.** *Let's read it again:* **This is a small clam.** *Which picture belongs with this sentence?* (the clam) *Draw a line to the clam.*

- *Now look at the first box at the bottom of the page. We are listening for the word that begins with /m/. Let's name the pictures together:* **ring, monkey.** *Which word begins with /m/:* **ring** *or* **monkey**? (monkey) *Circle the monkey. The word* **monkey** *begins with the letter* **m**.

- *Now look at the next box. We are going to circle the picture that ends with /m/. Let's say each picture name together:* **drum, book.** *Which word ends with /m/:* **drum** *or* **book**? (drum) *Circle the drum. The word* **drum** *ends with the letter* **m**.

Day 4 activity

SKILLS:
Phonemic Awareness
• Identify the initial or final phoneme of a spoken word

Literary Response and Analysis
• Participate in a group response to a literary selection, identifying the characters, setting, and sequence of events

Comprehension
• Make connections using prior knowledge and real-life experiences

Home–School Connection p. 66
Spanish version available (see p. 2)

Circle Activity

Have students sit in a circle. Then review the Day 1 story and connect it to students' lives by asking:

- *What did Grandpa make? Have you ever tasted a clam? What did it taste like?*

Have students practice distinguishing the initial and final **M** sound using the call-and-response activity below. Begin by having students sit cross-legged. Then teach them to respond to your call by patting their left knee when they say "first" and their right knee when they say "last." If necessary, place a sticker on students' left knee to help them remember right from left.

Recite the chant below as you alternate patting knees and clapping as you say each syllable.

Teacher: *Lis-ten, lis-ten, do you hear it?*
Let-ter **M**. *Let-ter* **M**.
Is it first, or is it last?
Tell me quick-ly, tell me fast: **mouse**!

Students: *First!* (pat left knee)

Teacher: *Clam!*

Students: *Last!* (pat right knee)

Repeat the chant using the following words: *moon, mitten, mask, make, arm, drum, worm, yum.*

Mm

Digging for Clams

Number the pictures in order.

Listen for It!

 <u>m</u>ouse

Circle the pictures that begin like **mouse**.

Pictures: *moon, mitten, fan, monkey*

Trace and write the letters.

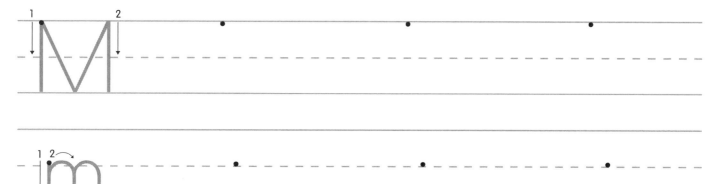

Read the sentence. Circle the word **mouse**.

This is a small mouse.

Name _____

Listen for It!

 clam

Circle the pictures that <u>end</u> like **clam**.

Pictures: *worm, bug, drum, farm*

Trace and write the letters.

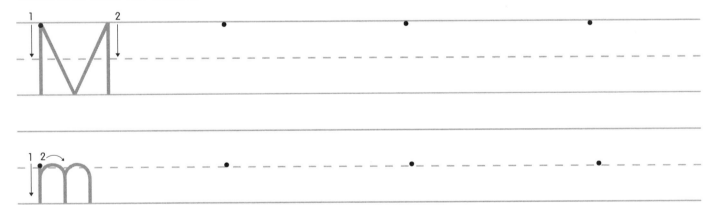

Read the sentence. Circle the word **clam**.

This is a small clam.

Everyday Literacy: Reading and Writing • EMC 2418 • © Evan-Moor Corp.

Name _____

Read It!

Read the sentence.
Draw a line to the correct picture.

This is a small mouse.   ★

This is a small clam.   ★

Circle the picture that begins with /**m**/.

Circle the picture that <u>ends</u> with /**m**/.

m_____

_____m

Pictures: *ring, monkey*

Pictures: *drum, book*

Name _____

Listen for the Sound of Mm

WEEK 7

Home–School Connection

To Parents

This week your child learned that **M** stands for the first sound in **mouse** and the last sound in **clam**.

Circle the pictures that <u>begin</u> with the same sound as **mouse**.

Underline the pictures that <u>end</u> with the same sound as **clam**.

<u>m</u>ouse | cla<u>m</u>

Pictures: *worm, mitten, drum, monkey, farm, moon*

Trace and write the letters.

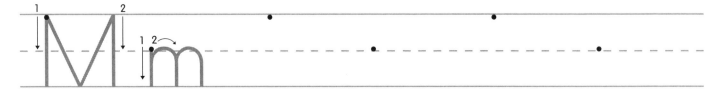

WEEK 8

Concept

Initial and Final
Sounds:

S, L, M

Review It

Vocabulary

Words with *s*, *l*, or *m* at the Beginning: seal, leaf, mouse

Words with *s*, *l*, or *m* at the End: octopus, owl, clam

High-Frequency Words: a, an, here, is, this

Day 1

SKILLS:
Concepts of Print
- Identify uppercase and lowercase letters

Phonemic Awareness
- Isolate and identify the initial phoneme of a spoken word

Phonics/Word Analysis
- Recognize that individual letters have associated sounds

Writing
- Print uppercase and lowercase letters
- Use spacing between letters and words when writing on a line

I Know *Ss, Ll,* and *Mm*

Distribute the Day 1 activity and a writing tool to each student. Then say:

- *Point to the seal. What is the first sound in **seal**? (/s/) What letter stands for /s/? (S) Point to the uppercase S. Trace it. Now point to the lowercase s. Trace it. Now write two uppercase Ss and two lowercase s's on the line.*

- *Point to the lion. What is the first sound in **lion**? (/l/) What letter stands for /l/? (L) Point to the uppercase L. Trace it. Now point to the lowercase l. Trace it. Now write two uppercase Ls and two lowercase l's on the line.*

Repeat the process for the remaining picture and letters. Then direct students' attention to the next task. Say:

- *Look at the uppercase alphabet at the bottom of the page. Let's name the letters together. (name aloud) Circle uppercase S, L, and M.*

- *Look at the lowercase alphabet below. Let's name the letters together. (name aloud) Now circle lowercase s, l, and m.*

Day 1 activity

Day 2

SKILLS:
Phonemic Awareness
- Identify the position of an isolated phoneme in a spoken word

Phonics/Word Analysis
- Learn and apply letter-sound correspondences
- Recognize that individual letters have associated sounds
- Read familiar CVC words and common sight words

Listening for *S, L,* and *M*

Distribute the Day 2 activity and a writing tool to each student. Then say:

- *We are going to listen for letter sounds. Point to the S row. What sound does S stand for? (/s/) Say **soap**. (soap) Do you hear /s/ first or last in **soap**? (first) Fill in the first circle under the soap. Say **octopus**. (octopus) Do you hear /s/ first or last in **octopus**? (last) Fill in the last circle. Say **dress**. (dress) Do you hear /s/ first or last in **dress**? (last) Fill in the last circle under the dress.*

- *Point to the L row. What sound does L stand for? (/l/) Say **leaf**. (leaf) Do you hear /l/ first or last in **leaf**? (first) Fill in the first circle under the leaf. Say **lamp**. Do you hear /l/ first or last in **lamp**? (first) Fill in the first circle. Say **hill**. Do you hear /l/ first or last in **hill**? (last) Fill in the last circle.*

Repeat the process for the remaining letter and pictures. Then direct students' attention to the next task. Say:

- *Point to the sentence at the bottom of the page. Move your finger under each word as you read it aloud. Now fill in the circle beside the matching picture.*

Day 2 activity

SKILLS:
Concepts of Print
- Understand that spoken words are represented in writing by specific sequences of letters

Phonological Awareness
- Identify and isolate the initial or final sound of a spoken word

Phonics/Word Analysis
- Learn and apply letter-sound correspondences
- Recognize that individual letters have associated sounds
- Read familiar CVC words and common sight words

Writing
- Write the letters that match sounds in words

Writing Words with *S, L,* and *M*

Distribute the Day 3 activity and a writing tool to each student. Say:

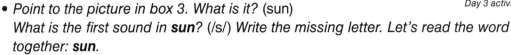

- *Each box shows a picture and a word that is missing a letter. We are going to say each picture name and write the missing letter. Point to the first picture. What is it? (mask) What is the first sound in* **mask***? (/m/) Write the missing letter. Now move your finger under each letter as we read the word together:* **mask***.*

- *Point to the picture in box 2. It shows rocks. What is the* <u>last</u> *sound in* **rocks***? (/s/) Write the missing letter. Let's read the word together:* **rocks***.*

- *Point to the picture in box 3. What is it? (sun) What is the first sound in* **sun***? (/s/) Write the missing letter. Let's read the word together:* **sun***.*

- *Point to the picture in box 4. What is it? (log) What is the first sound in* **log***? (/l/) Write the missing letter. Let's read the word together:* **log***.*

- *Point to the picture in box 5. What is it? (drum) What is the* <u>last</u> *sound in* **drum***? (/m/) Write the missing letter. Let's read the word together:* **drum***.*

- *Point to the picture in box 6. What is it? (owl) What is the* <u>last</u> *sound in* **owl***? (/l/) Write the missing letter. Let's read the word together:* **owl***.*

Day 3 activity

SKILLS:
Phonics/Word Analysis
- Learn and apply letter-sound correspondences
- Read familiar CVC words and common sight words

Comprehension
- Demonstrate comprehension of text read aloud by self or others

Reading Words with *S, L,* and *M*

Distribute the Day 4 activity and a writing tool to each student. Say:

- *Point to the first sentence. Move your finger under the words as we read together:* **This is a seal***. Draw a line from this sentence to the picture it matches.*

- *Point to sentence 2. Move your finger under the words as we read together:* **This is a mouse***. Draw a line from the sentence to the picture it matches.*

- *Point to sentence 3. Let's read it together:* **This is a lion***. Draw a line from the sentence to the picture it matches.*

- *Point to sentence 4. Let's read it together:* **This is an octopus***. Draw a line from the sentence to the picture it matches.*

- *Point to sentence 5. Let's read it together:* **This is a clam***. Draw a line from the sentence to the picture it matches.*

- *Point to sentence 6. Let's read it together:* **This is an owl***. Draw a line from the sentence to the picture it matches.*

Day 4 activity

SKILLS:

Phonemic Awareness

• Isolate and identify the initial or final phoneme of a spoken word

Phonics/Word Analysis

• Learn and apply letter-sound correspondences

• Recognize that individual letters have associated sounds

Home–School Connection p. 74
Spanish version available (see p. 2)

Phonics Review Game

Play the following game to review the initial and final consonant sounds that students learned this week.

Materials: 6 large index cards or 3 sheets of construction paper cut in half

Preparation: Write the letter **s** on two cards, the letter **l** on two cards, and the letter **m** on two cards. Divide the cards into two sets that contain one of each letter. Display one set of cards on each end of the board.

How to Play: Divide students into two teams. Have each team line up facing the board. Explain to students that you will say a word and that they should listen for the beginning sound. After you say the word, the first player in each line races up to the board, chooses the correct letter card, faces his or her team, and says the letter name aloud. Each correct answer is worth one point. The two players then return the cards to the ledge and go to the end of the line. Repeat the process until you have called all of the words in the chart below. The team with the most points wins. Play the game again, and have students listen for ending sounds.

Beginning Sounds:	Ending Sounds:
S: seal, sun, soap, sand, surprise	**S:** octopus, grass, dress, rocks, kiss
L: lion, light, listen, look, little	**L:** cool, hill, owl, bell, nail
M: mouse, moon, mitten, mask, mud	**M:** clam, arm, drum, worm, Sam

Name _____

Write It!

Trace then write each letter.

 S s

_____

- - - - - - - - - - - - - - - - - - -

_____

 L l

_____

- - - - - - - - - - - - - - - - - - -

_____

 M m

_____

- - - - - - - - - - - - - - - - - - -

_____

Find uppercase **S**, **L**, and **M**. Circle them.

A	B	C	D	E	F	G	H	I	J	K	L	M
N	O	P	Q	R	S	T	U	V	W	X	Y	Z

Find lowercase **s**, **l**, and **m**. Circle them.

a	b	c	d	e	f	g	h	i	j	k	l	m
n	o	p	q	r	s	t	u	v	w	x	y	z

Name _____

Listen for It!

Where do you hear the letter sound?
Fill in the circle to show **first** or **last**.

S s

L l

M m

Read the sentence.
Fill in the circle next to the correct picture.

Here is a fish.

Name _____

Spell It!

Say each picture name.
Write the missing letter.

s l m

1

 ___ ask

2

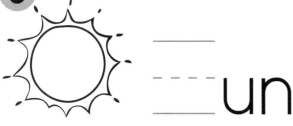 ___ rock

3

 ___ un

4

 ___ og

5

dru ___

6

ow ___

Everyday Literacy: Reading and Writing • EMC 2418 • © Evan-Moor Corp.

Name _____

Read It!

Read the sentence.
Draw a line to the correct picture.

1 This is a seal.

2 This is a mouse.

3 This is a lion.

4 This is an octopus.

5 This is a clam.

6 This is an owl.

Name _____

Beginning and Ending

Ss Ll Mm

WEEK 8

Home–School Connection

To Parents

This week your child reviewed beginning and ending sounds for the letters **S**, **L**, and **M**.

Name each picture. Draw a line to show what letter sound you hear at the **beginning**.

 •

 •

  •

s

l

m

Pictures: *sun, moon, lamp*

Name each picture. Draw a line to show what letter sound you hear at the **end**.

  •

   •

   •

s

l

m

Pictures: *owl, drum, dress*

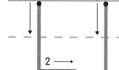

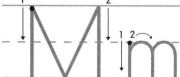

Everyday Literacy: Reading and Writing • EMC 2418 • © Evan-Moor Corp.

Dog Meets Toad

Concept: D stands for the first sound in **dog** and the last sound in **toad**.
High-Frequency Words: at, look, my

Day 1

SKILLS:

Concepts of Print
• Identify uppercase and lowercase letters of the alphabet

Phonemic Awareness
• Recognize a phoneme in a spoken word

Phonics/Word Analysis
• Learn and apply letter-sound correspondences
• Produce the sound a consonant letter makes in isolation

Literary Response and Analysis
• Participate in a group response to a literary selection, identifying the characters, setting, and sequence of events
• Make predictions about text content using pictures, background knowledge, and text features

Comprehension
• Answer questions about text read aloud
• Respond to who, what, where, why, how questions about text read aloud

Learning About the Letter *Dd*

Distribute the Day 1 activity page. Say: *This week's letter is **D**. Find **D** at the top of the page. Point to the uppercase **D**. Now point to the lowercase **d**. The letter **D** stands for this sound: /d/. Say /d/. (/d/) It is the first sound you hear in **dog**. Say **dog**. (dog) It is the last sound you hear in **toad**. Say **toad**. (toad) What sound does the letter **D** stand for? (/d/)*

Listening to the Story

To prepare students to listen to the story, say: *I am going to read you a story called "Dog Meets Toad." Look at the picture. What do you think happens in the story? (students respond) Listen for the /d/ sound as I read the story.*

One **day**, **Danny** the **dog** chased a **bird** all the way to the **pond**. He ran and ran until he felt **mud** under his paws. Then Danny started to **dig**. Suddenly, a **toad** jumped up out of the mud. "Can't a toad take a nap?" it croaked. Danny looked at the toad in surprise. "I'm tired during the day because I'm up all night catching insects," said the toad. "I'm tired, too," said Danny. "I've been chasing a bird. I'd like to take a nap, too." So Danny laid next to the toad and they fell asleep.

Thinking About the Story

Distribute crayons or markers. Guide students in answering questions about the story. Say:

Day 1 picture

• *Look at the big picture. What does Danny like to do at the pond? (dig in the mud) Do you hear /d/ in **dig**? (yes) Do you hear /d/ in **mud**? (yes) Make a brown dot on the mud.*

• *Who woke the toad? (Danny the dog) Do you hear /d/ in **dog**? (yes) Do you hear /d/ in **Danny**? (yes) Make a blue dot on Danny the dog.*

• *What did Danny find in the mud? (a toad) Do you hear /d/ in **toad**? (yes) Make a green dot on the toad.*

• *What made Danny the dog tired? (He chased a bird.) Circle the bird.*

• *The little pictures at the bottom of the page show what happened in the story. What happened first? (dog starts to dig) Write **1** under the picture.*

• *What happened next? (toad jumps out of the mud) Write **2** under the picture.*

• *What happened last? (dog and toad take a nap) Write **3** under the picture.*

Day 2

SKILLS:

Concepts of Print

- Locate a printed word on a page
- Follow words from top to bottom and left to right
- Track print by pointing to written words when text is read aloud by self or others

Phonemic Awareness

- Segment the initial phoneme of a spoken word

Phonics/Word Analysis

- Learn and apply letter-sound correspondences

Writing

- Print uppercase and lowercase letters
- Use spacing between letters and words when writing on a line

Reading and Writing Initial *D*

Distribute the Day 2 activity and a writing tool. Say:

- *Yesterday we read a story about a dog. Point to the dog at the top of the page. Say **dog**. (dog) What is the first sound in **dog**? (/d/) What letter stands for /d/? (D) Let's read the word **dog** together. Put your finger under the letter **d**. Move your finger under the word as you read it with me: **dog**.*

- *Now look at the pictures in the box. We're going to circle the pictures that begin with /d/. Point to the dime. Say **dime**. (dime) Does **dime** begin with /d/? (yes) Draw a circle around the dime.*

Repeat the process for the remaining pictures. Then direct students' attention to the next task. Say:

Day 2 activity

- *We are going to write uppercase **D** and lowercase **d**. Start at the black dot on uppercase **D**. Trace the line down. Go to the black dot again. Trace the line around the curve. Go to the next black dot. Write another uppercase **D**.*

Guide students through writing two more uppercase **D**s. Then say:

- *Now let's write lowercase **d**. Start at the black dot. Trace the line around to make a circle. Go to the top of the line beside the number 2. Trace the line down. Now write three more lowercase **d**'s.*

- *Look at the sentence at the bottom of the page. It says **Look at my dog**. Move your finger under each word as you read it with me: **Look at my dog**. Circle the word **dog**.*

Day 3

SKILLS:

Concepts of Print

- Locate a printed word on a page
- Follow words from top to bottom and left to right
- Track print by pointing to written words when text is read aloud by self or others

Phonemic Awareness

- Segment the final phoneme of a spoken word

Phonics/Word Analysis

- Learn and apply letter-sound correspondences

Writing

- Print uppercase and lowercase letters
- Use spacing between letters and words when writing on a line

Reading and Writing Final *D*

Distribute the Day 3 activity and a writing tool. Say:

- *The toad in our story liked to sleep in the mud. Point to the toad at the top of the page. Say **toad**. (toad) What is the last sound in **toad**? (/d/) What letter stands for /d/? (D) Let's read the word **toad** together. Put your finger under the letter **t**. Move your finger under the word as you read it with me: **toad**.*

- *Now look at the pictures in the box. We're going to circle the pictures that end with /d/. Put your finger on the bird. Say **bird**. (bird) Does **bird** end with /d/? (yes) Draw a circle around the bird.*

Repeat the process for the remaining pictures. Then direct students' attention to the next task. Say:

Day 3 activity

- *Yesterday we followed the dots and the arrows to write uppercase and lowercase **D**s. We are going to do it again today. Trace the uppercase **D**. Then start at each dot and write an uppercase **D**.*

- *Now trace the lowercase **d**. Then start at each dot and write a lowercase **d**.*

- *Look at the sentence at the bottom of the page. It says **Look at my toad**. Move your finger under each word as you read it with me: **Look at my toad**. Circle the word **toad**.*

Everyday Literacy: Reading and Writing • EMC 2418 • © Evan-Moor Corp.

Day 4

SKILLS:

Concepts of Print

• Locate a printed word on a page

Phonemic Awareness

• Identify the initial or final phoneme of a spoken word

Phonics/Word Recognition

• Recognize that individual letters have associated sounds

Literary Response and Analysis

• Participate in a group response to a literary selection, identifying the characters, setting, and sequence of events

Comprehension

• Answer questions about text read aloud

• Respond to *who, what, where, why, how* questions about text read aloud

Initial and Final *D*

Reread the Day 1 story. Then guide a discussion about the story by saying:

The title of this week's story is "Dog Meets Toad."

• *What was the setting of the story?* (the pond)

• *Why was the toad sleeping during the day?* (It stays awake at night to catch insects.)

• *Why was Danny the dog tired?* (He chased a bird.)

Then distribute the Day 4 activity and a writing tool. Say:

• *Point to the first sentence. Move your finger under each word as we read together:* **Look at my dog.** *Let's read it again:* **Look at my dog.** *Which picture belongs with this sentence?* (the dog) *Draw a line from the sentence to the dog.*

• *Point to the next sentence. Move your finger under each word as we read together:* **Look at my toad.** *Let's read it again:* **Look at my toad.** *Which picture belongs with this sentence?* (the toad) *Draw a line from the sentence to the toad.*

• *Now look at the first box at the bottom of the page. We are listening for the word that begins with /d/. Let's name the pictures together:* **duck, bell.** *Which word begins with /d/:* **duck** *or* **bell**? (duck) *Circle the duck. The word* **duck** *begins with the letter* **d.**

• *Now look at the next box. We are going to circle the picture that ends with /d/. Let's say each picture name together:* **cat, bird.** *Which word ends with /d/:* **cat** *or* **bird**? (bird) *Circle the bird. The word* **bird** *ends with the letter* **d.**

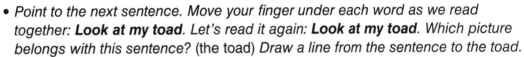

Day 4 activity

Day 5

SKILLS:

Phonemic Awareness

• Identify the initial or final phoneme of a spoken word

Literary Response and Analysis

• Participate in a group response to a literary selection, identifying the characters, setting, and sequence of events

Comprehension

• Make connections using prior knowledge and real-life experiences

Home–School Connection p. 82

Spanish version available (see p. 2)

Circle Activity

Have students sit in a circle. Then review the Day 1 story and connect it to students' lives by asking:

• *What animals were in the story?*

• *Do you or does someone you know have a dog or a toad?*

• *What was real in the story? What was make-believe?*

Have students practice distinguishing the initial and final **D** sound using the call-and-response activity below. Begin by having students sit cross-legged. Then teach them to respond to your call by patting their left knee when they say "first" and their right knee when they say "last." If necessary, place a sticker on students' left knee to help them remember right from left.

Recite the chant below as you alternate patting knees and clapping as you say each syllable.

Teacher: *Lis-ten, lis-ten, do you hear it?*
Let-ter **D.** *Let-ter* **D.**
Is it first, or is it last?
Tell me quick-ly, tell me fast: **dog**!

Students: *First!* (pat left knee)

Teacher: *Toad!*

Students: *Last!* (pat right knee)

Repeat the chant using the following words: *dig, dime, dinosaur, bird, sled, pond.*

Dd

Dog Meets Toad

Number the pictures in order.

Name _____

Listen for It!  <u>d</u>og

Circle the pictures that begin like **dog**.

Pictures: *dime, donut, pig, dinosaur*

Trace and write the letters.

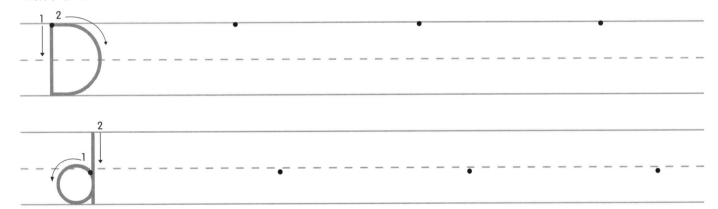

Read the sentence. Circle the word **dog**.

Look at my dog.

Listen for It!

 toad

Circle the pictures that <u>end</u> like **toad**.

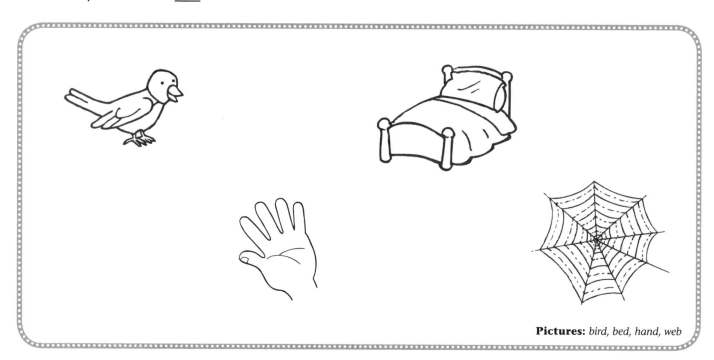

Pictures: *bird, bed, hand, web*

Trace and write the letters.

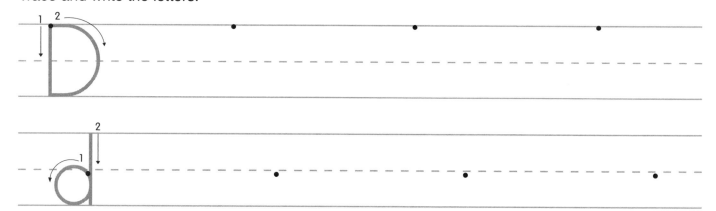

Read the sentence. Circle the word **toad**.

Look at my toad.

Everyday Literacy: Reading and Writing • EMC 2418 • © Evan-Moor Corp.

Name _____

Read It!

Read the sentence.
Draw a line to the correct picture.

Look at my dog.   ★

Look at my toad.   ★

Circle the picture that begins with **/d/**.

Circle the picture that ends with **/d/**.

d _____

Pictures: *duck, bell*

_____ **d**

Pictures: *cat, bird*

© Evan-Moor Corp. • EMC 2418 • *Everyday Literacy: Reading and Writing*   Week 9   **81**

Name _____

Listen for the Sound of Dd

Circle the pictures that <u>begin</u> with the same sound as **dog.**

Underline the pictures that <u>end</u> with the same sound as **toad.**

WEEK 9

Home–School Connection

To Parents

This week your child learned that **D** stands for the first sound in **dog** and the last sound in **toad**.

<u>d</u>og

toa<u>d</u>

Pictures: *duck, hand, bird, dinosaur, dime, bed*

Trace and write the letters.

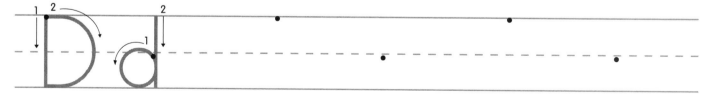

Everyday Literacy: Reading and Writing • EMC 2418 • © Evan-Moor Corp.

A Happy Tune

Concept: N stands for the first sound in **nest** and the last sound in **hen**.
High-Frequency Words: see, the, we

Day 1

SKILLS:
Concepts of Print
• Identify uppercase and lowercase letters of the alphabet

Phonemic Awareness
• Recognize a phoneme in a spoken word

Phonics/Word Analysis
• Learn and apply letter-sound correspondences
• Produce the sound a consonant letter makes in isolation

Literary Response and Analysis
• Participate in a group response to a literary selection, identifying the characters, setting, and sequence of events
• Make predictions about text content using pictures, background knowledge, and text features

Comprehension
• Answer questions about text read aloud
• Respond to *who, what, where, why, how* questions about text read aloud

Learning About the Letter *Nn*

Distribute the Day 1 activity page. Say: *This week's letter is **N**. Find **N** at the top of the page. Point to the uppercase **N**. Now point to the lowercase **n**. The letter **N** stands for this sound: **/n/**. Say **/n/**. (/n/) It is the first sound you hear in **nest**. Say **nest**. (nest) It is the last sound you hear in **hen**. Say **hen**. (hen) What sound does the letter **N** stand for? (/n/)*

Listening to the Story

To prepare students to listen to the story, say: *I am going to read you a story. The title is "A Happy Tune." Look at the picture. What do you think happens in the story? (students respond) Listen for the **/n/** sound as I read the story.*

---

*My morning was filled with music. First, I heard a bird singing "tweet-tweet-tweet" in its **nest**. Its song told the other birds to keep away. **Next**, I heard the **hen** rapping "cluck-cluck-cluck." She was calling her baby chicks to come and eat the seeds that were scattered in the yard. **Then**, I heard my mom humming the **notes** of a happy tune while she cooked in the **kitchen**. That was the music I liked best, because it told me breakfast was almost ready!*

Thinking About the Story

Distribute crayons or markers. Guide students in answering questions about the story. Say:

Day 1 picture

• *Look at the big picture. Why did the bird sing? (to tell other birds to stay away from its nest) Do you hear **/n/** in **nest**? (yes) Make a brown dot on the nest.*

• *Why did the hen cluck? (calling chicks to eat) Do you hear **/n/** in **hen**? (yes) Make a yellow dot on each chick.*

• *Why did the girl like her mom's music best? (because it told her breakfast was almost ready) Make a red dot on the girl's mom.*

• *The little pictures at the bottom of the page show us how the girl's morning was filled with music. What did the girl hear first? (bird singing in its nest) Write **1** under the picture.*

• *What did she hear next? (hen clucking) Write **2** under the picture.*

• *What did she hear last? (mom humming) Write **3** under the picture.*

SKILLS:

Concepts of Print
- Locate a printed word on a page
- Follow words from top to bottom and left to right
- Track print by pointing to written words when text is read aloud by self or others

Phonemic Awareness
- Segment the initial phoneme of a spoken word

Phonics/Word Analysis
- Learn and apply letter-sound correspondences

Writing
- Print uppercase and lowercase letters
- Use spacing between letters and words when writing on a line

Reading and Writing Initial *N*

Distribute the Day 2 activity and a writing tool. Say:

- *Yesterday we read a story about a bird singing in a nest. Point to the nest at the top of the page. Say* **nest**. *(nest) What is the first sound in* **nest**? *(/n/) What letter stands for /n/?* (N) *Let's read the word* **nest** *together. Put your finger under the letter* **n**. *Move your finger under the word as you read it with me:* **nest**.

- *Now look at the pictures in the box. We're going to circle the pictures that* <u>begin</u> *with /n/. Point to the nail. Say* **nail**. *(nail) Does* **nail** *begin with /n/? (yes) Draw a circle around the nail.*

Repeat the process for the remaining pictures. Then direct students' attention to the next task. Say:

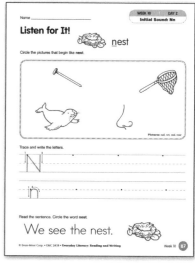

Day 2 activity

- *We are going to write uppercase* **N** *and lowercase* **n**. *Start at the black dot on uppercase* **N**. *Trace the line down. Go to the black dot again. Trace the other line down and follow the last line up. Go to the next black dot. Write another uppercase* **N**.

Guide students through writing two more uppercase Ns. Then say:

- *Now let's write lowercase* **n**. *Start at the black dot. Trace the line down. Go to the black dot again. Follow the line over and down. Now write three more lowercase* **n**'s.

- *Look at the sentence at the bottom of the page. It says* **We see the nest**. *Move your finger under each word as you read it with me:* **We see the nest**. *Circle the word* **nest**.

SKILLS:

Concepts of Print
- Locate a printed word on a page
- Follow words from top to bottom and left to right
- Track print by pointing to written words when text is read aloud by self or others

Phonemic Awareness
- Segment the final phoneme of a spoken word

Phonics/Word Analysis
- Learn and apply letter-sound correspondences

Writing
- Print uppercase and lowercase letters
- Use spacing between letters and words when writing on a line

Reading and Writing Final *N*

Distribute the Day 3 activity and a writing tool. Say:

- *The hen in this week's story called her baby chicks to come and eat. Point to the hen at the top of the page. Say* **hen**. *(hen) What is the* <u>last</u> *sound in* **hen**? *(/n/) What letter stands for /n/?* (N) *Let's read the word* **hen** *together. Put your finger under the letter* **h**. *Move your finger under the word as you read it with me:* **hen**.

- *Now look at the pictures in the box. We're going to circle the pictures that* <u>end</u> *with /n/. Put your finger on the train. Say* **train**. *(train) Does* **train** *end with /n/? (yes) Draw a circle around the train.*

Repeat the process for the remaining pictures. Then direct students' attention to the next task. Say:

Day 3 activity

- *Yesterday we followed the dots and the arrows to write uppercase and lowercase* **N**s. *We are going to do it again today. Trace the uppercase* **N**. *Then start at each dot and write an uppercase* **N**.

- *Now trace the lowercase* **n**. *Then start at each dot and write a lowercase* **n**.

- *Look at the sentence at the bottom of the page. It says* **We see the hen**. *Move your finger under each word as you read it with me:* **We see the hen**. *Circle the word* **hen**.

SKILLS:

Concepts of Print
• Locate a printed word on a page

Phonemic Awareness
• Identify the initial or final phoneme of a spoken word

Phonics/Word Recognition
• Recognize that individual letters have associated sounds

Literary Response and Analysis
• Participate in a group response to a literary selection, identifying the characters, setting, and sequence of events

Comprehension
• Answer questions about text read aloud
• Respond to *who, what, where, why, how* questions about text read aloud

Initial and Final *N*

Reread the Day 1 story. Then guide a discussion about the story by saying:

This week's story was about a girl who heard music all around her.

• *Which animals made music?* (bird, hen)

• *How did the bird make music?* (it sang)

• *How did the mom make music?* (she hummed)

Then distribute the Day 4 activity and a writing tool. Say:

• *Point to the first sentence. Move your finger under each word as we read together: **We see the nest**. Let's read it again: **We see the nest**. Draw a line to the picture that belongs with this sentence.*

• *Point to the next sentence. Move your finger under each word as we read together: **We see the hen**. Let's read it again: **We see the hen**. Draw a line to the picture that belongs with this sentence.*

• *Now look at the first box at the bottom of the page. We are listening for the word that begins with /n/. Let's name the pictures together: **boat, nail**. Which word begins with /n/: **boat** or **nail**?* (nail) *Circle the nail. The word **nail** begins with the letter **n**.*

• *Now look at the next box. We are going to circle the picture that ends with /n/. Let's say each picture name together: **owl, fan**. Which word ends with /n/: **owl** or **fan**?* (fan) *Circle the fan. The word **fan** ends with the letter **n**.*

Day 4 activity

SKILLS:

Phonemic Awareness
• Identify the initial or final phoneme of a spoken word

Literary Response and Analysis
• Participate in a group response to a literary selection, identifying the characters, setting, and sequence of events

Comprehension
• Make connections using prior knowledge and real-life experiences

Home–School Connection p. 90
Spanish version available (see p. 2)

Circle Activity

Have students sit in a circle. Then review the Day 1 story and connect it to students' lives by asking:

• *Who or what makes music at your house?*

• *Do you ever hum or sing?*

Have students practice distinguishing the initial and final **N** sound using the call-and-response activity below. Begin by having students sit cross-legged. Then teach them to respond to your call by patting their left knee when they say "first" and their right knee when they say "last." If necessary, place a sticker on students' left knee to help them remember right from left.

Recite the chant below as you alternate patting knees and clapping as you say each syllable.

Teacher: *Lis-ten, lis-ten, do you hear it?*
*Let-ter **N**. Let-ter **N**.*
Is it first, or is it last?
*Tell me quick-ly, tell me fast: **nest**!*

Students: *First!* (pat left knee)

Teacher: *Hen!*

Students: *Last!* (pat right knee)

Repeat the chant using the following words: *nose, nurse, train, can, lion.*

Name _____

Nn

A Happy Tune

Number the pictures in order.

Name _____

Listen for It!

 <u>n</u>est

Circle the pictures that begin like **nest**.

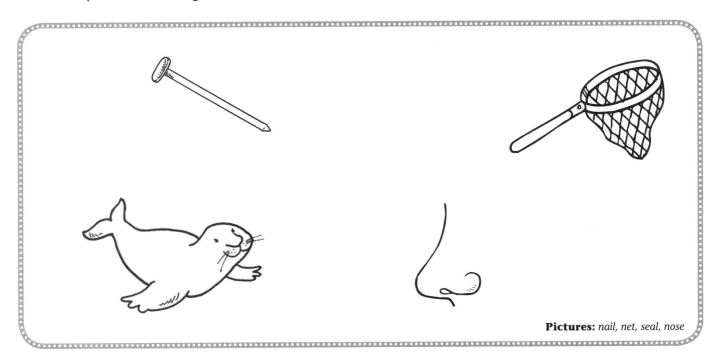

Pictures: *nail, net, seal, nose*

Trace and write the letters.

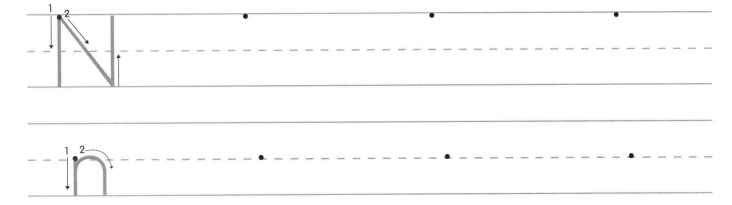

Read the sentence. Circle the word **nest**.

We see the nest.

Name _____

Listen for It!

 he<u>n</u>

Circle the pictures that <u>end</u> like **hen**.

Pictures: *train, fan, cake, lion*

Trace and write the letters.

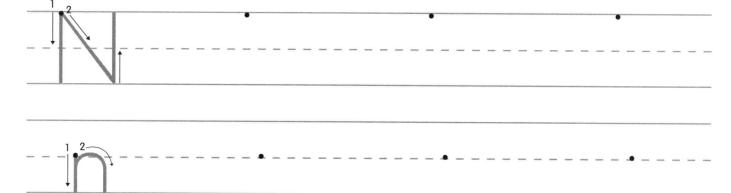

Read the sentence. Circle the word **hen**.

We see the hen.

Everyday Literacy: Reading and Writing • EMC 2418 • © Evan-Moor Corp.

Name _____

Read It!

Read the sentence.
Draw a line to the correct picture.

We see the nest.

★

We see the hen.

★

Circle the picture that begins with **/n/**.

n____

Pictures: *boat, nail*

Circle the picture that <u>ends</u> with **/n/**.

____n

Pictures: *owl, fan*

Name _____

Listen for the Sound of Nn

WEEK 10

Home–School Connection

To Parents

This week your child learned that **N** stands for the first sound in **nest** and the last sound in **hen**.

Circle the pictures that <u>begin</u> with the same sound as **nest**.

Underline the pictures that <u>end</u> with the same sound as **hen**.

nest | hen

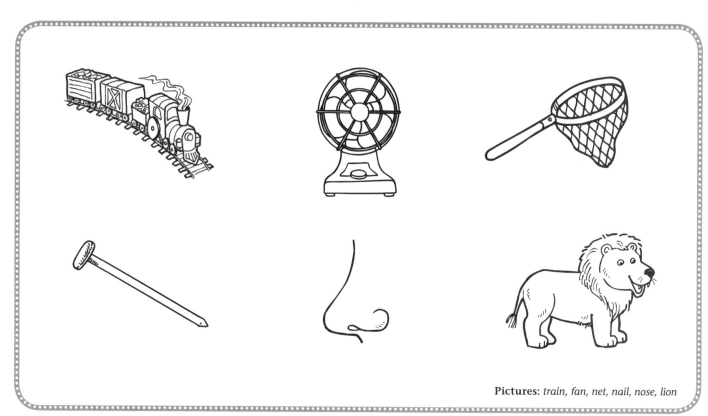

Pictures: *train, fan, net, nail, nose, lion*

Trace and write the letters.

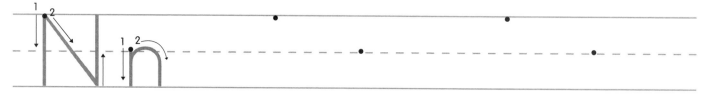

Everyday Literacy: Reading and Writing • EMC 2418 • © Evan-Moor Corp.

A Curious Goat

Concept: T stands for the first sound in **turtle** and the last sound in **goat**.
High-Frequency Words: a, is, it

Learning About the Letter *Tt*

Distribute the Day 1 activity page. Say: *This week's letter is **T**. Find **T** at the top of the page. Point to the uppercase **T**. Now point to the lowercase **t**. The letter **T** stands for this sound: /t/. Say /t/. (/t/) It is the first sound you hear in **turtle**. Say **turtle**. (turtle) It is the <u>last</u> sound you hear in **goat**. Say **goat**. (goat) What sound does the letter **T** stand for? (/t/)*

Listening to the Story

To prepare students to listen to the story, say: *I am going to read you a story. The title is "A Curious Goat." Look at the picture. What do you think happens in the story? (students respond) Listen for the /t/ sound as I read the story.*

---

*I'm a **goat**, and like most goats, I'm curious. I nibble on things that I'm curious about. I'm curious about children. They like to **pet** my **soft** wool. I like to nibble on their jacket buttons or **take** a bite out of their straw **hats**. One day, I was giving some children a ride in my little **cart**, when I saw a big rock in the road. I stopped. The rock moved. It wasn't a rock after all. It was a **turtle**! When I inched closer to have a nibble, the turtle snapped at my nose! I moved just in **time**. I learned that sometimes being curious can be dangerous—especially if you **meet** a turtle!*

Thinking About the Story

Distribute crayons or markers. Guide students in answering questions about the story. Say:

Day 1 picture

• *Look at the big picture. What do goats do when they are curious about something? (nibble on it) Do you hear /t/ in **goat**? (yes) Make a brown dot on the goat.*

• *What did the big rock turn out to be? (a turtle) Do you hear /t/ in **turtle**? (yes) Make a green dot on the turtle.*

• *Look at the little pictures at the bottom of the page. Let's number the pictures in the order that they happened in the story. What happened first? (the goat pulled a cart) Write **1** under the picture.*

• *What happened next? (goat saw a turtle) Write **2** under the picture.*

• *What happened last? (turtle snapped at goat) Write **3** under the picture.*

Day 2

SKILLS:

Concepts of Print

- Locate a printed word on a page
- Follow words from top to bottom and left to right
- Track print by pointing to written words when text is read aloud by self or others

Phonemic Awareness

- Segment the initial phoneme of a spoken word

Phonics/Word Analysis

- Learn and apply letter-sound correspondences

Writing

- Print uppercase and lowercase letters
- Use spacing between letters and words when writing on a line

Reading and Writing Initial *T*

Distribute the Day 2 activity and a writing tool. Say:

- *Yesterday we read a story about a turtle that snapped at a goat. Point to the turtle at the top of the page. Say* **turtle**. *(turtle) What is the first sound in* **turtle**? */(t/) What letter stands for* **/t/**? *(T) Let's read the word* **turtle** *together. Put your finger under the letter* **t**. *Move your finger under the word as you read it with me:* **turtle**.

- *Now look at the pictures in the box. We're going to circle the pictures that <u>begin with</u> /t/. Point to the tire. Say* **tire**. *(tire) Does* **tire** *begin with /t/? (yes) Draw a circle around the tire.*

Repeat the process for the remaining pictures. Then direct students' attention to the next task. Say:

- *We are going to write uppercase* **T** *and lowercase* **t**. *Start at the black dot on uppercase* **T**. *Trace the line down. Then trace the line below the number 2 across. Go to the next black dot. Write another uppercase* **T**.

Guide students through writing two more uppercase Ts. Then say:

- *Now let's write lowercase* **t**. *Start at the black dot. Trace the line down. Go to the line above the number 2. Follow the line across. Now write three more lowercase* **t**'*s.*

- *Look at the sentence at the bottom of the page. It says* **It is a turtle**. *Move your finger under each word as you read it with me:* **It is a turtle**. *Circle the word* **turtle**.

Day 2 activity

Day 3

SKILLS:

Concepts of Print

- Locate a printed word on a page
- Follow words from top to bottom and left to right
- Track print by pointing to written words when text is read aloud by self or others

Phonemic Awareness

- Segment the final phoneme of a spoken word

Phonics/Word Analysis

- Learn and apply letter-sound correspondences

Writing

- Print uppercase and lowercase letters
- Use spacing between letters and words when writing on a line

Reading and Writing Final *T*

Distribute the Day 3 activity and a writing tool. Say:

- *This week's story was about a curious goat. Point to the goat at the top of the page. Say* **goat**. *(goat) What is the <u>last</u> sound in* **goat**? */(t/) What letter stands for* **/t/**? *(T) Let's read the word* **goat** *together. Put your finger under the letter* **g**. *Move your finger under the word as you read it with me:* **goat**.

- *Now look at the pictures in the box. We're going to circle the pictures that <u>end</u> with /t/. Put your finger on the jet. Say* **jet**. *(jet) Does* **jet** *end with /t/? (yes) Draw a circle around the jet.*

Repeat the process for the remaining pictures. Then direct students' attention to the next task. Say:

- *Yesterday we followed the dots and the arrows to write uppercase and lowercase* **T**s. *We are going to do it again today. Trace the uppercase* **T**. *Then start at each dot and write an uppercase* **T**.

- *Now trace the lowercase* **t**. *Then start at each dot and write a lowercase* **t**.

- *Look at the sentence at the bottom of the page. It says* **It is a goat**. *Move your finger under each word as you read it with me:* **It is a goat**. *Circle the word* **goat**.

Day 3 activity

Day 4

SKILLS:

Concepts of Print
- Locate a printed word on a page

Phonemic Awareness
- Identify the initial or final phoneme of a spoken word

Phonics/Word Recognition
- Recognize that individual letters have associated sounds

Literary Response and Analysis
- Participate in a group response to a literary selection, identifying the characters, setting, and sequence of events

Comprehension
- Answer questions about text read aloud
- Respond to *who, what, where, why, how* questions about text read aloud

Initial and Final *T*

Reread the Day 1 story. Then guide a discussion about the story by saying:

Our story this week was called "A Curious Goat."

- *The word "curious" means you want to find out more or learn more about something. What was the goat curious about?* (children, a turtle)

- *What did the turtle do to the curious goat?* (snapped at its nose)

Then distribute the Day 4 activity and a writing tool. Say:

- *Point to the first sentence. Move your finger under each word as we read together: **It is a turtle**. Let's read it again: **It is a turtle**. Which picture belongs with this sentence?* (the turtle) *Draw a line from the sentence to the turtle.*

- *Point to the next sentence. Move your finger under each word as we read together: **It is a goat**. Let's read it again: **It is a goat**. Which picture belongs with this sentence?* (the goat) *Draw a line from the sentence to the goat.*

- *Now look at the first box at the bottom of the page. We are listening for the word that <u>begins</u> with /t/. Let's name the pictures together: **tire, monkey**. Which word begins with /t/: **tire** or **monkey**?* (tire) *Circle the tire. The word **tire** begins with the letter **t**.*

- *Now look at the next box. We are going to circle the picture that <u>ends</u> with /t/. Let's say each picture name together: **drum, jet**. Which word ends with /t/: **drum** or **jet**?* (jet) *Circle the jet. The word **jet** ends with the letter **t**.*

Day 4 activity

Day 5

SKILLS:

Phonemic Awareness
- Identify the initial or final phoneme of a spoken word

Literary Response and Analysis
- Participate in a group response to a literary selection, identifying the characters, setting, and sequence of events

Comprehension
- Make connections using prior knowledge and real-life experiences

Home–School Connection p. 98
Spanish version available (see p. 2)

Circle Activity

Have students sit in a circle. Then review the Day 1 story and connect it to students' lives by asking:

- *Who were the characters in this week's story? What were they doing?*

- *Have you ever seen or touched a goat or a turtle? Where were you?*

Have students practice distinguishing the initial and final **T** sound using the call-and-response activity below. Begin by having students sit cross-legged. Then teach them to respond to your call by patting their left knee when they say "first" and their right knee when they say "last." If necessary, place a sticker on students' left knee to help them remember right from left.

Recite the chant below as you alternate patting knees and clapping as you say each syllable.

Teacher: *Lis-ten, lis-ten, do you hear it?*
*Let-ter **T**. Let-ter **T**.*
Is it first, or is it last?
*Tell me quick-ly, tell me fast: **turtle**!*

Students: *First!* (pat left knee)

Teacher: *Goat!*

Students: *Last!* (pat right knee)

Repeat the chant using the following words: *tire, top, turkey, pet, boat, foot.*

Name _____

Tt

A Curious Goat

Number the pictures in order.

( ) ( ) ( )

Name _____

Listen for It!

 <u>t</u>urtle

Circle the pictures that begin like **turtle**.

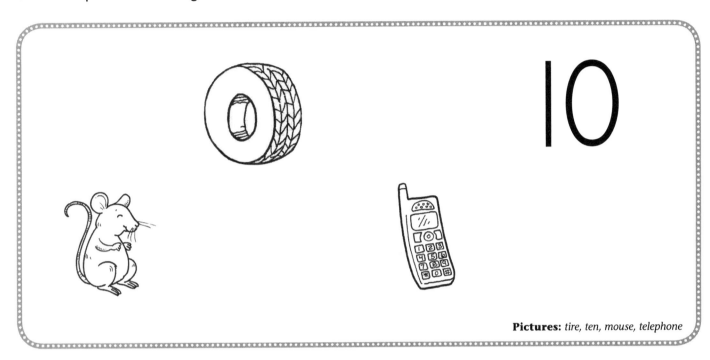

Pictures: *tire, ten, mouse, telephone*

Trace and write the letters.

Read the sentence. Circle the word **turtle**.

It is a turtle.

© Evan-Moor Corp. • EMC 2418 • *Everyday Literacy: Reading and Writing*   Week 11   95

Name _____

Listen for It!

 goa<u>t</u>

Circle the pictures that <u>end</u> like **goat**.

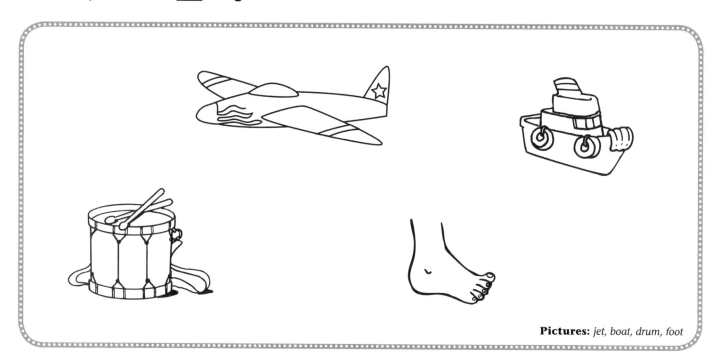

Pictures: *jet, boat, drum, foot*

Trace and write the letters.

Read the sentence. Circle the word **goat**.

It is a goat.

Everyday Literacy: Reading and Writing • EMC 2418 • © Evan-Moor Corp.

Name _____

Read It!

Read the sentence.
Draw a line to the correct picture.

It is a turtle.

★

It is a goat.

★

Circle the picture that begins with /t/.

t _____

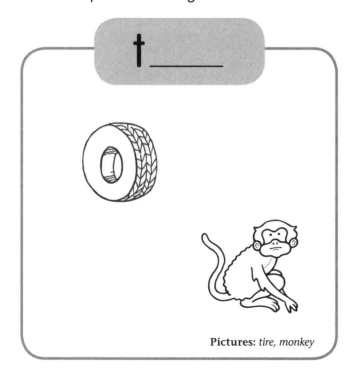

Pictures: *tire, monkey*

Circle the picture that <u>ends</u> with /t/.

_____ t

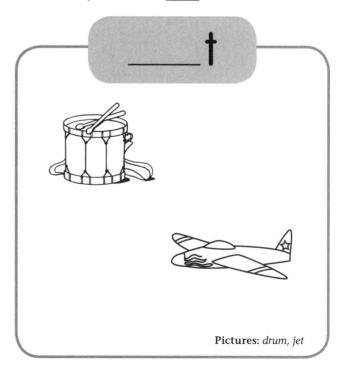

Pictures: *drum, jet*

© Evan-Moor Corp. • EMC 2418 • **Everyday Literacy: Reading and Writing**

Name _____

Listen for the Sound of Tt

WEEK 11

Home–School Connection

To Parents

This week your child learned that **T** stands for the first sound in **turtle** and the last sound in **goat**.

Circle the pictures that <u>begin</u> with the same sound as **turtle**.

Underline the pictures that <u>end</u> with the same sound as **goat**.

turtle | goat

Pictures: *tire, ten, boat, telephone, jet, foot*

Trace and write the letters.

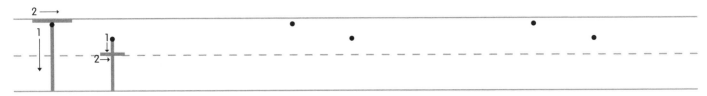

Everyday Literacy: Reading and Writing • EMC 2418 • © Evan-Moor Corp.

Review It

Concept

Initial and Final Sounds:

D, N, T

Vocabulary

Words with *d*, *n*, or *t* at the Beginning: dinosaur, dog, duck, nail, nest, net, ten, turkey, turtle

Words with *d*, *n*, or *t* at the End: bed, bird, fan, hat, hen, jet, lion, moon, train

High-Frequency Words: at, is, it, look, my, the, we

Day 1

SKILLS:
Concepts of Print
• Identify uppercase and lowercase letters of the alphabet

Phonemic Awareness
• Isolate and identify the initial or final phoneme of a spoken word

Phonics/Word Analysis
• Recognize that individual letters have associated sounds

Writing
• Print uppercase and lowercase letters
• Use spacing between letters and words when writing on a line

I Know *Dd*, *Nn*, and *Tt*

Distribute the Day 1 activity and a writing tool to each student. Then say:

• *Point to the dog. What is the first sound in **dog**? (/d/) What letter stands for /d/? (D) Point to the uppercase **D**. Trace it. Now point to the lowercase **d**. Trace it. Now write two uppercase **D**s and two lowercase **d**'s on the line.*

• *Point to the nest. What is the first sound in **nest**? (/n/) What letter stands for /n/? (N) Point to the uppercase **N**. Trace it. Now point to the lowercase **n**. Trace it. Now write two uppercase **N**s and two lowercase **n**'s on the line.*

Repeat the process for the remaining picture and letters. Then direct students' attention to the next task. Say:

• *Look at the uppercase alphabet at the bottom of the page. Let's name the letters together. (name aloud) Circle uppercase **D**, **N**, and **T**.*

• *Look at the lowercase alphabet below. Let's name the letters together. (name aloud) Now circle lowercase **d**, **n**, and **t**.*

Day 1 activity

Day 2

SKILLS:
Phonemic Awareness
• Identify the position of an isolated phoneme in a spoken word

Phonics/Word Analysis
• Learn and apply letter-sound correspondences
• Recognize that individual letters have associated sounds
• Read familiar CVC words and common sight words

Listening for *Dd*, *Nn*, and *Tt*

Distribute the Day 2 activity and a writing tool to each student. Then say:

• *We are going to listen for letter sounds. Point to the **D** row. What sound does **D** stand for? (/d/) Say **bird**. (bird) Do you hear /d/ first or last in **bird**? (last) Fill in the last circle under the bird. Say **duck**. (duck) Do you hear /d/ first or last in **duck**? (first) Fill in the first circle under the duck. Say **dinosaur**. (dinosaur) Do you hear /d/ first or last in **dinosaur**? (first) Fill in the first circle under the dinosaur.*

• *Point to the **N** row. What sound does **N** stand for? (/n/) Say **nail**. (nail) Do you hear /n/ first or last in **nail**? (first) Fill in the first circle under the nail. Say **train**. (train) Do you hear /n/ first or last in **train**? (last) Fill in the last circle. Say **moon**. (moon) Do you hear /n/ first or last in **moon**? (last) Fill in the last circle.*

Repeat the process for the remaining letter and pictures. Then direct students' attention to the next task. Say:

• *Point to the sentence at the bottom of the page. Move your finger under each word as you read it aloud. Now fill in the circle beside the matching picture.*

Day 2 activity

Day 3

Writing Words with *D, N,* and *T*

Distribute the Day 3 activity and a writing tool to each student. Say:

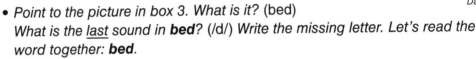
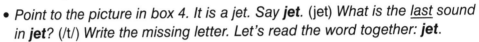

Day 3 activity

- *Each box shows a picture and a word that is missing a letter. We are going to say each picture name and write the missing letter. Point to the first picture. What is it?* (dog) *What is the first sound in* **dog**? (/d/) *Write the missing letter. Now move your finger under each letter as we read the word together:* **dog**.

- *Point to the picture in box 2. What is it?* (net) *What is the first sound in* **net**? (/n/) *Write the missing letter. Let's read the word together:* **net**.

- *Point to the picture in box 3. What is it?* (bed) *What is the* <u>last</u> *sound in* **bed**? (/d/) *Write the missing letter. Let's read the word together:* **bed**.

- *Point to the picture in box 4. It is a jet. Say* **jet**. (jet) *What is the* <u>last</u> *sound in* **jet**? (/t/) *Write the missing letter. Let's read the word together:* **jet**.

- *Point to the picture in box 5. What is it?* (fan) *What is the* <u>last</u> *sound in* **fan**? (/n/) *Write the missing letter. Let's read the word together:* **fan**.

- *Point to the picture in box 6. What is it?* (the number ten) *What is the first sound in* **ten**? (/t/) *Write the missing letter. Let's read the word together:* **ten**.

Day 4

Reading Words with *D, N,* and *T*

Distribute the Day 4 activity and pencils or crayons. Then say:

Day 4 activity

- *Point to the first sentence. Move your finger under the words as we read together:* **We look at the nest**. *Draw a line from this sentence to the picture it matches.*

- *Point to sentence 2. Move your finger under the words as we read together:* **We look at the goat**. *Draw a line from the sentence to the picture it matches.*

- *Point to sentence 3. Let's read it together:* **We look at the hen**. *Draw a line from the sentence to the picture it matches.*

- *Point to sentence 4. Let's read it together:* **We look at the turtle**. *Draw a line from the sentence to the picture it matches.*

- *Point to sentence 5. Let's read it together:* **We look at the dog**. *Draw a line from the sentence to the picture it matches.*

- *Point to sentence 6. Let's read it together:* **We look at the bird**. *Draw a line from the sentence to the picture it matches.*

SKILLS:
Phonemic Awareness
• Isolate and identify the initial or final phoneme of a spoken word

Phonics/Word Analysis
• Learn and apply letter-sound correspondences
• Recognize that individual letters have associated sounds

Home–School Connection p. 106
Spanish version available (see p. 2)

Phonics Review Game

Play the following game to review the initial and final consonant sounds that students have learned this week.

Materials: 6 large index cards or 3 pieces of construction paper cut in half

Preparation: Write the letter **d** on two cards, the letter **n** on two cards, and the letter **t** on two cards. Divide the cards into two sets that contain one of each letter. Display one set of cards on each end of the board.

How to Play: Divide students into two teams. Have each team line up facing the board. Explain to students that you will say a word and that they should listen for the beginning sound. After you say the word, the first player in each line races up to the board, chooses the correct letter card, faces his or her team, and says the letter name aloud. Each correct answer is worth one point. The two players then return the cards to the ledge and go to the end of the line. Repeat the process until you have called all of the words in the chart below. The team with the most points wins. Play the game again, and have students listen for ending sounds.

Beginning Sounds:	Ending Sounds:
D: Danny, dime, dig, dog, dinosaur **N:** nest, nail, night, note, nose **T:** take, time, turtle, turkey, top	**D:** bird, mud, pond, toad, sled **N:** hen, kitchen, then, train, can **T:** cart, goat, hat, pet, soft

Name _____

Write It!

Trace then write each letter.

 Dd _____

 Nn _____

 Tt _____

Find uppercase **D**, **N**, and **T**. Circle them.

A	B	C	D	E	F	G	H	I	J	K	L	M
N	O	P	Q	R	S	T	U	V	W	X	Y	Z

Find lowercase **d**, **n**, and **t**. Circle them.

a	b	c	d	e	f	g	h	i	j	k	l	m
n	o	p	q	r	s	t	u	v	w	x	y	z

Everyday Literacy: Reading and Writing • EMC 2418 • © Evan-Moor Corp.

Name _____

Listen for It!

Where do you hear the letter sound?
Fill in the circle to show **first** or **last**.

Read the sentence.
Fill in the circle next to the correct picture.

It is my dog.

Name _____

Spell It!

Say each picture name.
Write the missing letter.

d n t

1

 __ og

2

 __ et

3

 be __

4

 je __

5

fa __

6

10 __ en

Everyday Literacy: Reading and Writing • EMC 2418 • © Evan-Moor Corp.

Name _____

Read It!

Read the sentence.
Draw a line to the correct picture.

1 We look at the nest.

2 We look at the goat.

3 We look at the hen.

4 We look at the turtle.

5 We look at the dog.

6 We look at the bird.

Name _____

Beginning and Ending

Dd Nn Tt

WEEK 12

Home–School Connection

To Parents

This week your child reviewed beginning and ending sounds for the letters **D**, **N**, and **T**.

Name each picture. Draw a line to show what letter sound you hear at the **beginning**.

d

n

t

Name each picture. Draw a line to show what letter sound you hear at the **end**.

d

n

t

Pictures: *turtle, duck, nest*

Pictures: *bird, goat, hen*

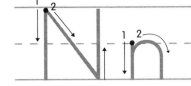

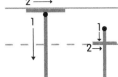

Everyday Literacy: Reading and Writing • EMC 2418 • © Evan-Moor Corp.

June Bug Dances

Concept: J stands for the first sound in **June** Bug.
High-Frequency Words: a, can, do, he, she, they

Learning About the Letter *Jj*

Distribute the Day 1 activity page. Say: *This week's letter is J. Find J at the top of the page. Point to the uppercase J. Now point to the lowercase j. The letter J stands for this sound: /j/. Say /j/. (/j/) It is the first sound you hear in June. Say June. (June) What sound does the letter J stand for? (/j/)*

Listening to the Story

To prepare students to listen to the story, say: *I am going to read you a story. The title is "June Bug Dances." Look at the picture. What do you think happens in the story? (students respond) Listen for the /j/ sound as I read the story.*

As **June** Bug **jumped** through the garden one summer evening, she heard music and singing. Now, if there is anything June Bug loves, it's music. When she hears it, she **just** has to dance a **jig**! So June Bug followed the sound of the music, and before long, she came upon garden creatures having a party. A blue **jay** was singing, crickets were chirping, and grasshoppers were dancing in the grass. June Bug **joined** the party. She jumped onto a daisy and danced a jig!

Thinking About the Story

Distribute crayons or markers. Guide students in answering questions about the story. Say:

• *What is the title of the story?* (June Bug Dances)

• *Look at the big picture. Who danced a jig in the story?* (June Bug) *Do you hear /j/ in **jig**?* (yes) *Do you hear /j/ in **June**?* (yes) *Make a red dot on June Bug dancing a jig.*

• *Who was singing?* (a blue jay) *Do you hear /j/ in **jay**?* (yes) *Make a blue dot on the blue jay.*

• *Look at the little pictures at the bottom of the page. Let's number the pictures in the order that they happened in the story. What did June Bug hear?* (music and singing) *Write 1 under the picture of June Bug listening.*

• *What happened next?* (June Bug came upon the party.) *Write 2 under the picture of the party.*

• *What happened at the end of the story?* (June Bug jumped onto a daisy and danced a jig.) *Write 3 under the picture of June Bug dancing a jig.*

Day 1 picture

Day 2

SKILLS:

Concepts of Print

- Locate a printed word on a page
- Follow words from top to bottom and left to right
- Track print by pointing to written words when text is read aloud by self or others

Phonemic Awareness

- Segment the initial phoneme of a spoken word

Phonics/Word Analysis

- Learn and apply letter-sound correspondences

Writing

- Print uppercase and lowercase letters
- Use spacing between letters and words when writing on a line

Reading and Writing Initial *J*

Distribute the Day 2 activity and a writing tool. Say:

- *Yesterday we read a story about June Bug dancing a jig. Point to June Bug at the top of the page. Say* **jig***. (jig) What is the first sound in* **jig***? (/j/) What letter stands for* /j/*? (J) Let's read the word* **jig** *together. Put your finger under the letter* **j***. Move your finger under the word as you read it with me:* **jig***.*

- *Now look at the pictures in the box. We're going to circle the pictures that begin with* /j/*. Point to the bird. This is a blue jay. Say* **jay***. (jay) Does* **jay** *begin with* /j/*? (yes) Draw a circle around the blue jay.*

Repeat the process for the remaining pictures. Then direct students' attention to the next task. Say:

- *We are going to write uppercase* **J** *and lowercase* **j***. Start at the black dot on uppercase* **J***. Trace the line down and follow the curve up. Go to the next black dot. Write another uppercase* **J***.*

Guide students through writing two more uppercase Js. Then say:

- *Now let's write lowercase* **j***. Start at the black dot. Trace the line down and follow the curve up. Now trace the dot at the top. Write three more lowercase* **j***'s.*

- *Look at the sentence at the bottom of the page. It says* **She can do a jig***. Move your finger under each word as you read it with me:* **She can do a jig***. Circle the word* **jig***.*

Day 2 activity

Day 3

SKILLS:

Concepts of Print

- Locate a printed word on a page
- Follow words from top to bottom and left to right
- Track print by pointing to written words when text is read aloud by self or others

Phonemic Awareness

- Recognize a phoneme in a spoken word

Comprehension

- Make connections using prior knowledge and real-life experiences

Writing

- Print uppercase and lowercase letters
- Use spacing between letters and words when writing on a line

Listening for Initial *J*

Reread the Day 1 story. Then guide a discussion about the story by saying:

Our story was about garden creatures having a party. Is this story real or make-believe? Explain what parts are real and what parts are make-believe. (answers vary)

Distribute the Day 3 activity and a writing tool. Say:

- *This week we are learning about the letter* **J***. What sound does the letter* **J** *stand for? (/j/)*

- *Point to the jeep in box 1. Say* **jeep***. (jeep) Do you hear* /j/ *in* **jeep***? (yes) Color the happy face for* **yes***.*

- *Point to the house. Say* **house***. (house) Do you hear* /j/ *in* **house***? (no) Color the happy face for* **yes** *or the sad face for* **no***.*

- *Point to the juice box. Say* **juice***. (juice) Do you hear* /j/ *in* **juice***? (yes) Color the happy face for* **yes** *or the sad face for* **no***.*

- *Point to the jar. Say* **jar***. (jar) Do you hear* /j/ *in* **jar***? (yes) Color the happy face for* **yes***.*

- *Now point to June Bug from this week's story. What is she doing? (dancing a jig) Point to the word* **jig***. Move your finger under the word as we read it together:* **jig***. Trace the word* **jig** *and then write it on the next line.*

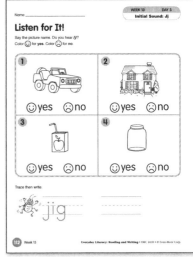

Day 3 activity

SKILLS:

Concepts of Print
- Locate a printed word on a page

Phonemic Awareness
- Identify the initial phoneme of a spoken word

Phonics/Word Recognition
- Recognize that individual letters have associated sounds

Literary Response and Analysis
- Participate in a group response to a literary selection, identifying the characters, setting, and sequence of events

Comprehension
- Answer questions about text read aloud
- Respond to *who, what, where, why, how* questions about text read aloud

Reading and Writing with Initial J

Reread the Day 1 story. Then guide a discussion about the story by saying:

Our story this week was "June Bug Dances."

- *Which two ways did June Bug move in the story?* (She jumped and she danced a jig.)
- *What animal was singing?* (blue jay)
- *What animal was chirping?* (cricket)

Then distribute the Day 4 activity and a writing tool. Say:

- *Point to the first sentence. Move your finger under each word as we read together:* **She can do a jig.** *Let's read it again:* **She can do a jig.** *Which picture belongs with this sentence?* (June Bug) *Draw a line to June Bug.*
- *Point to the next sentence. Move your finger under each word as we read together:* **He can do a jig.** *Let's read it again:* **He can do a jig.** *Which picture belongs with this sentence?* (the grasshopper) *Draw a line to the grasshopper.*
- *Point to the last sentence. Move your finger under each word as we read together:* **They can do a jig.** *Let's read it again:* **They can do a jig.** *Which picture belongs with this sentence?* (June Bug and the grasshopper) *Draw a line to June Bug and the grasshopper doing a jig.*
- *Now we are going to write uppercase* **J** *and lowercase* **j**. *Let's start with uppercase* **J**. *Start at the black dot, trace the line down, and follow the curve up. Write three more uppercase Js.*
- *Now let's write lowercase* **j**. *Start at the black dot. Trace the line down and follow the curve up. Now trace the dot at the top. Write three more lowercase j's.*

Day 4 activity

SKILLS:

Phonemic Awareness
- Identify the initial phoneme of a spoken word

Literary Response and Analysis
- Participate in a group response to a literary selection, identifying the characters, setting, and sequence of events

Comprehension
- Make connections using prior knowledge and real-life experiences

Home–School Connection p. 114
Spanish version available (see p. 2)

Circle Activity

Have students sit in a circle. Then review the Day 1 story and connect it to students' lives by asking:

- *What season is it in the story? Summer or winter?*
- *Have you ever seen a jumping insect? Tell us about it.*

Have students practice distinguishing the initial **J** sound using the call-and-response activity below. Begin by having students sit cross-legged. Then teach them to respond to your call by patting their left knee when they say "yes" and their right knee when they say "no." If necessary, place a sticker on students' left knee to help them remember right from left.

Recite the chant below as you alternate patting knees and clapping as you say each syllable.

Teacher: *Lis-ten, lis-ten, do you hear it?*
Let-ter **J**. *Let-ter* **J**. *It says /j/. It says /j/.*
Do you hear it? Yes or no?
Lis-ten: **June**!

Students: *Yes!* (pat left knee)

Teacher: **Nest**!

Students: *No!* (pat right knee)

Repeat the chant using the following words: *jam, jiggle, juice, jog.*

Name _____

Jj

June Bug Dances

Number the pictures in order.

Name _____

Listen for It!

<u>j</u>ig

Circle the pictures that begin like **jig**.

Pictures: *jay, jump, jet, goose*

Trace and write the letters.

J

j

Read the sentence. Circle the word **jig**.

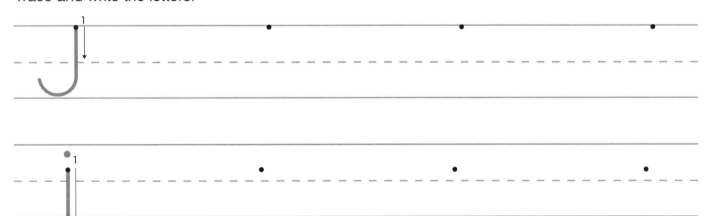

She can do a jig.

Listen for It!

Say the picture name. Do you hear **/j/**?
Color 😊 for **yes**. Color 🙁 for **no**.

1 😊 yes   🙁 no

2 😊 yes   🙁 no

3 😊 yes   🙁 no

4 😊 yes   🙁 no

Trace then write.

jig

Name _____

Read It!

Read the sentence.
Draw a line to the correct picture.

She can do a jig. ★

He can do a jig. ★

They can do a jig. ★

Trace and write the letters.

Name _____

Listen for the Sound of Jj

Circle the pictures that begin with the same sound as **jig**.

WEEK 13

Home–School Connection

To Parents

This week your child learned that **J** stands for the first sound in **jig**.

 jig

Pictures: *jet, jar, cub, jam, pig*

Trace and write the letters.

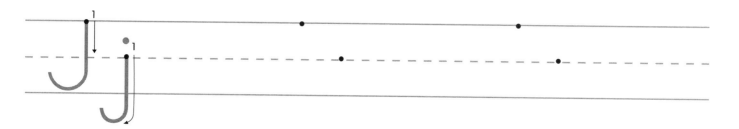

Everyday Literacy: Reading and Writing • EMC 2418 • © Evan-Moor Corp.

Look in a Book

Concept: **K** stands for the first sound in **kangaroo** and the last sound in **yak**.
High-Frequency Words: a, are, you

Day 1

SKILLS:
Concepts of Print
• Identify uppercase and lowercase letters of the alphabet
Phonemic Awareness
• Recognize a phoneme in a spoken word
Phonics/Word Analysis
• Learn and apply letter-sound correspondences
• Produce the sound a consonant letter makes in isolation
Literary Response and Analysis
• Participate in a group response to a literary selection, identifying the characters, setting, and sequence of events
• Make predictions about text content using pictures, background knowledge, and text features
Comprehension
• Answer questions about text read aloud
• Respond to *who, what, where, why, how* questions about text read aloud

Learning About the Letter *Kk*

Distribute the Day 1 activity page. Say: *This week's letter is* **K**. *Find* **K** *at the top of the page. Point to the uppercase* **K**. *Now point to the lowercase* **k**. *The letter* **K** *stands for this sound:* **/k/**. *Say* **/k/**. *(/k/) It is the first sound you hear in* **kangaroo**. *Say* **kangaroo**. *(kangaroo) It is the* last *sound you hear in* **yak**. *Say* **yak**. *(yak) What sound does the letter* **K** *stand for? (/k/)*

Listening to the Story

To prepare students to listen to the story, say: *I am going to read you a story. The title is "Look in a Book." Look at the picture. What do you think happens in the story? (students respond) Listen for the* **/k/** *sound as I read the story.*

---

*Have you ever looked in a **book** to learn about something? I **look** in a book to learn how to make a **kite**. I look in a book to learn how to make a pizza. I look in a book to learn about animals like a **kangaroo** and a **yak**. Books teach me with pictures and words. I learn a lot about the world. Books are really fun. I bet if you look in a book, you will learn a lot, too. What book do you want to look at?*

Thinking About the Story

Distribute crayons or markers. Guide students in answering questions about the story. Say:

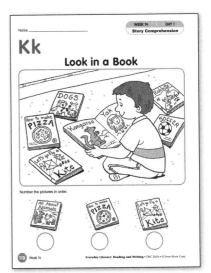

Day 1 picture

• *What is the title of the story? (Look in a Book) Do you hear* **/k/** *in* **look**? *(yes) Do you hear* **/k/** *in* **book**? *(yes)*

• *Look at the big picture. Why does the boy look at books? (to learn) What do the pages of a book have on them? (pictures and words) Make a blue dot on the book you would like to look at.*

• *Look at the little pictures at the bottom of the page. What did the boy tell us he learned about first? (kite) Write* **1** *under the picture that shows a book about a kite.*

• *What did the boy tell us he learned about next? (pizza) Write* **2** *under the picture that shows a book about pizza.*

• *What did the boy tell us he learned about last? (kangaroo and yak) Write* **3** *under the picture that shows a book about a kangaroo and a yak.*

SKILLS:

Concepts of Print

- Locate a printed word on a page
- Follow words from top to bottom and left to right
- Track print by pointing to written words when text is read aloud by self or others

Phonemic Awareness

- Segment the initial phoneme of a spoken word

Phonics/Word Analysis

- Learn and apply letter-sound correspondences

Writing

- Print uppercase and lowercase letters
- Use spacing between letters and words when writing on a line

Reading and Writing Initial *K*

Distribute the Day 2 activity and a writing tool. Say:

- *Yesterday we read a story about a boy who looked in a book to learn about a kangaroo. Point to the kangaroo at the top of the page. Say* **kangaroo**. *(kangaroo) What is the first sound in* **kangaroo**? *(/k/) What letter stands for* **/k/**? *(K) Let's read the word* **kangaroo** *together. It is a long word with a lot of letters. Put your finger under the letter* **k**. *Move your finger under the word as you read it with me:* **kangaroo**.

- *Now look at the pictures in the box. We're going to circle the pictures that begin with* **/k/**. *Point to the key. Say* **key**. *(key) Does* **key** *begin with* **/k/**? *(yes) Draw a circle around the key.*

Day 2 activity

Repeat the process for the remaining pictures. Then direct students' attention to the next task. Say:

- *We are going to write uppercase* **K** *and lowercase* **k**. *Start at the black dot on uppercase* **K**. *Trace the line down. Go to the line beside the number 2. Trace it down and down again. Go to the next black dot. Write another uppercase* **K**.

Guide students through writing two more uppercase Ks. Then say:

- *Now let's write lowercase* **k**. *Start at the black dot. Trace the line down. Go to the line below the number 2. Follow the line down and down again. Now write three more lowercase* **k**'s.

- *Look at the sentence at the bottom of the page. It says* **Are you a kangaroo?** *This sentence asks a question. Move your finger under each word as you read the question with me:* **Are you a kangaroo?** *Circle the* **k** *in* **kangaroo**.

SKILLS:

Concepts of Print

- Locate a printed word on a page
- Follow words from top to bottom and left to right
- Track print by pointing to written words when text is read aloud by self or others

Phonemic Awareness

- Segment the final phoneme of a spoken word

Phonics/Word Analysis

- Learn and apply letter-sound correspondences

Writing

- Print uppercase and lowercase letters
- Use spacing between letters and words when writing on a line

Reading and Writing Final *K*

Distribute the Day 3 activity and a writing tool. Say:

- *The boy in our story looked in a book to learn about a yak. Point to the yak at the top of the page. Say* **yak**. *(yak) What is the* last *sound in* **yak**? *(/k/) What letter stands for* **/k/**? *(K) Let's read the word* **yak** *together. Put your finger under the letter* **y**. *Move your finger under the word as you read it with me:* **yak**.

- *Now look at the pictures in the box. We're going to circle the pictures that* end *with* **/k/**. *Put your finger on the book. Say* **book**. *(book) Does* **book** *end with* **/k/**? *(yes) Draw a circle around the book.*

Day 3 activity

Repeat the process for the remaining pictures. Then direct students' attention to the next task. Say:

- *Yesterday we followed the dots and the arrows to write uppercase and lowercase* **K**s. *We are going to do it again today. Trace the uppercase* **K**. *Then start at each dot and write an uppercase* **K**.

- *Now trace the lowercase* **k**. *Then start at each dot and write a lowercase* **k**.

- *Look at the sentence at the bottom of the page. It says* **Are you a yak?** *Move your finger under each word as you read the question with me:* **Are you a yak?** *Circle the word* **yak**.

SKILLS:

Concepts of Print
- Locate a printed word on a page

Phonemic Awareness
- Identify the initial or final phoneme of a spoken word

Phonics/Word Recognition
- Recognize that individual letters have associated sounds

Literary Response and Analysis
- Participate in a group response to a literary selection, identifying the characters, setting, and sequence of events

Comprehension
- Answer questions about text read aloud
- Respond to *who, what, where, why, how* questions about text read aloud

Initial and Final *K*

Reread the Day 1 story. Then guide a discussion about the story by saying:

The boy in our story likes books.

- *What book did the boy look in to learn how to make pizza?* (the pizza book)
- *How does the boy learn about the world?* (by reading/looking in books)
- *What question does the boy ask at the end of the story?* (What book do you want to look at?)

Then distribute the Day 4 activity and a writing tool. Say:

- *Point to the first sentence. It says* **Are you a kangaroo?** *This sentence asks a question. Move your finger under each word as we read together:* **Are you a kangaroo?** *Let's read it again:* **Are you a kangaroo?** *Which picture belongs with this sentence?* (kangaroo) *Draw a line to the correct picture.*

- *Point to the next sentence. Move your finger under each word as we read together:* **Are you a yak?** *Let's read it again:* **Are you a yak?** *Does this sentence ask a question?* (yes) *Draw a line to the picture that belongs with this sentence.*

- *Now look at the first box at the bottom of the page. We are listening for the word that begins with* /k/. *Let's name the pictures together:* **kite, leaf.** *Which word begins with* /k/: **kite** *or* **leaf**? (kite) *Circle the kite. The word* **kite** *begins with the letter* **k.**

- *Now look at the next box. We are going to circle the picture that* <u>ends</u> *with* /k/. *Let's say each picture name together:* **pig, sock.** *Which word ends with* /k/: **pig** *or* **sock**? (sock) *Circle the sock. The word* **sock** *ends with the letter* **k.**

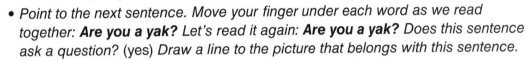

Day 4 activity

SKILLS:

Phonemic Awareness
- Identify the initial or final phoneme of a spoken word

Literary Response and Analysis
- Participate in a group response to a literary selection, identifying the characters, setting, and sequence of events

Comprehension
- Make connections using prior knowledge and real-life experiences

Home–School Connection p. 122
Spanish version available (see p. 2)

Circle Activity

Have students sit in a circle. Then review the Day 1 story and connect it to students' lives by asking:

- *Does the boy in our story like books?*
- *Do you have books of your own? Have you ever looked in a book to learn?*

Have students practice distinguishing the initial and final **K** using the call-and-response activity below. Begin by having students sit cross-legged. Then teach them to respond to your call by patting their left knee when they say "first" and their right knee when they say "last." If necessary, place a sticker on students' left knee to help them remember right from left.

Recite the chant below as you alternate patting knees and clapping as you say each syllable.

Teacher: *Lis-ten, lis-ten, do you hear it?*
Let-ter **K.** *Let-ter* **K.**
Is it first, or is it last?
Tell me quick-ly, tell me fast: **kite**!

Students: *First!* (pat left knee)

Teacher: *Yak!*

Students: *Last!* (pat right knee)

Repeat the chant using the following words: *king, key, kitten, block, book, lock.*

Name _____

Kk

Look in a Book

Number the pictures in order.

◯   ◯   ◯

Everyday Literacy: Reading and Writing • EMC 2418 • © Evan-Moor Corp.

Name _____

Listen for It!

 <u>k</u>angaroo

Circle the pictures that begin like **kangaroo**.

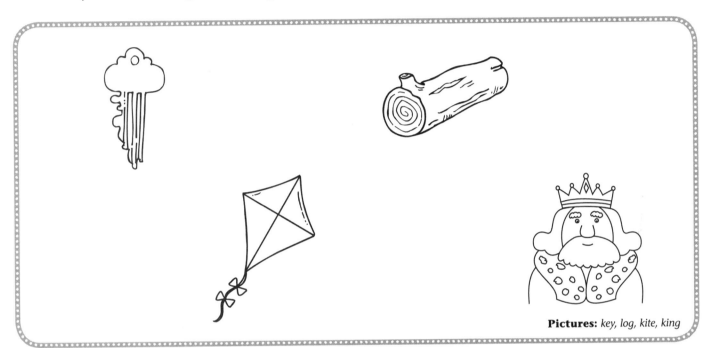

Pictures: *key, log, kite, king*

Trace and write the letters.

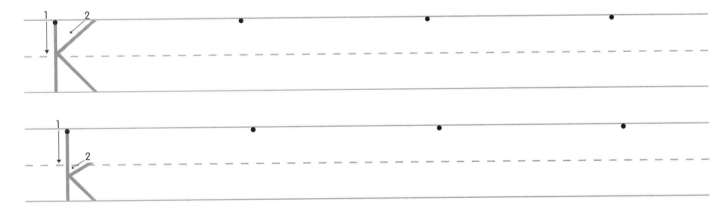

Read the sentence. Circle the **k** in **kangaroo**.

Are you a kangaroo?

Name _____

Listen for It!

 ya<u>k</u>

Circle the pictures that <u>end</u> like **yak**.

Pictures: *book, block, sock, pig*

Trace and write the letters.

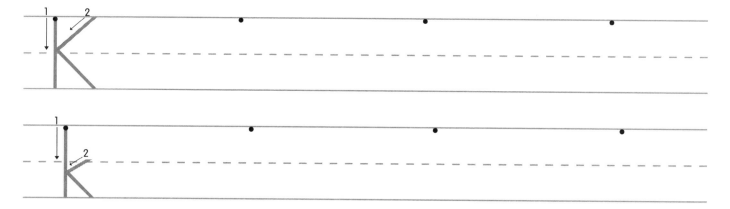

Read the sentence. Circle the word **yak**.

Are you a yak?

Everyday Literacy: Reading and Writing • EMC 2418 • © Evan-Moor Corp.

Name _____

Read It!

Read the sentence.
Draw a line to the correct picture.

Are you a kangaroo?   ★

Are you a yak?   ★

Circle the picture that begins with /k/.

k___

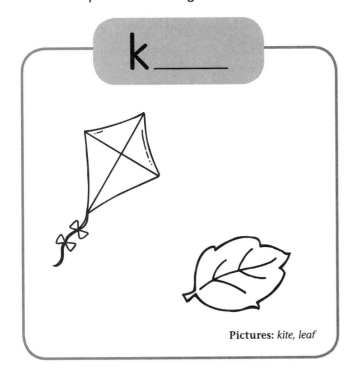

Pictures: *kite, leaf*

Circle the picture that <u>ends</u> with /k/.

___k

Pictures: *pig, sock*

Name _____

Listen for the Sound of **K k**

Circle the pictures that <u>begin</u> with the same sound as **kangaroo**.

Underline the pictures that <u>end</u> with the same sound as **yak**.

WEEK 14

Home–School Connection

To Parents

This week your child learned that **K** stands for the first sound in **kangaroo** and the last sound in **yak**.

<u>k</u>angaroo | **ya<u>k</u>**

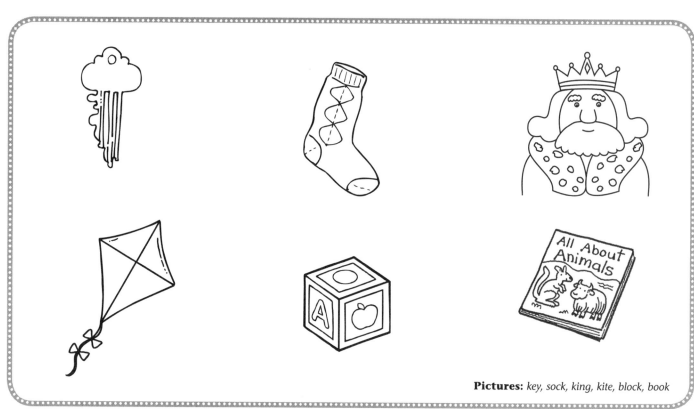

Pictures: *key, sock, king, kite, block, book*

Trace and write the letters.

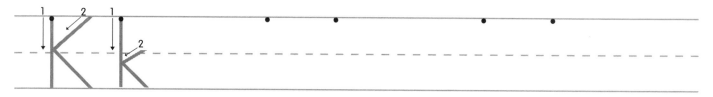

Rabbit Hops Away

Concept: R stands for the first sound in **rabbit** and the last sound in **spider**.
High-Frequency Words: can, go, this

Day 1

SKILLS:

Concepts of Print
- Identify uppercase and lowercase letters of the alphabet

Phonemic Awareness
- Recognize a phoneme in a spoken word

Phonics/Word Analysis
- Learn and apply letter-sound correspondences
- Produce the sound a consonant letter makes in isolation

Literary Response and Analysis
- Participate in a group response to a literary selection, identifying the characters, setting, and sequence of events
- Make predictions about text content using pictures, background knowledge, and text features

Comprehension
- Answer questions about text read aloud
- Respond to *who, what, where, why, how* questions about text read aloud

Learning About the Letter *Rr*

Distribute the Day 1 activity page. Say: *This week's letter is **R**. Find **R** at the top of the page. Point to the uppercase **R**. Now point to the lowercase **r**. The letter **R** stands for this sound: **Irl**. Say **Irl**. (/r/) It is the first sound you hear in **rabbit**. Say **rabbit**. (rabbit) It is the last sound you hear in **spider**. Say **spider**. (spider) What sound does the letter **R** stand for? (/r/)*

Listening to the Story

To prepare students to listen to the story, say: *I am going to read you a story. The title is "Rabbit Hops Away." Look at the picture. What do you think happens in the story? (students respond) Listen for the **Irl** sound as I read the story.*

*It was a sunny day in Mrs. **Ryan's** garden. A large **spider** finished spinning a web. A **rabbit** squeezed under the fence and hopped into the garden looking for vegetables. The spider watched the rabbit nibble on a small carrot. The spider knew that Mrs. Ryan did not like rabbits in her garden. Just as the rabbit finished eating the carrot, Mrs. Ryan's dog **Rover** woke up from a nap and sniffed the **air**. He let out a loud bark and took off **running** toward the rabbit. The rabbit quickly hopped across the garden and squeezed **under** the fence. The spider said, "Wow! I'm glad I only eat bugs. Eating vegetables is dangerous!"*

Thinking About the Story

Distribute crayons or markers. Guide students in answering questions about the story. Say:

- *Remember, the place where the story happens is called the **setting**. What is the setting of this story?* (Mrs. Ryan's garden)

- *Who was looking for vegetables to eat?* (the rabbit) *Do you hear **Irl** in **rabbit**?* (yes) *Make a blue dot on the rabbit.*

- *Who was watching the rabbit nibble on a carrot?* (the spider) *Do you hear **Irl** in **spider**?* (yes) *Make a brown dot on the spider.*

- *Look at the pictures at the bottom of the page. Let's number the pictures in the order that they happened in the story. What happened first?* (spider made a web) *Write **1** under the picture.*

- *What happened next?* (rabbit ate a carrot) *Write **2** under the picture.*

- *What happened last?* (dog chased the rabbit away) *Write **3** under the picture.*

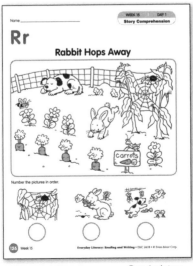

Day 1 picture

SKILLS:
Concepts of Print
- Locate a printed word on a page
- Follow words from top to bottom and left to right
- Track print by pointing to written words when text is read aloud by self or others

Phonemic Awareness
- Segment the initial phoneme of a spoken word

Phonics/Word Analysis
- Learn and apply letter-sound correspondences

Writing
- Print uppercase and lowercase letters
- Use spacing between letters and words when writing on a line

Reading and Writing Initial *R*

Distribute the Day 2 activity and a writing tool. Say:

- *Yesterday's story was about a rabbit in a garden. Point to the rabbit at the top of the page. Say* **rabbit***. (rabbit) What is the first sound in* **rabbit***? (/r/) What letter stands for /r/? (R) Let's read the word* **rabbit** *together. Put your finger under the letter* **r***. Move your finger under the word as you read it with me:* **rabbit***.*

- *Now look at the pictures in the box. We're going to circle the pictures that begin with /r/. Point to the ring. Say* **ring***. (ring) Does* **ring** *begin with /r/? (yes) Draw a circle around the ring.*

Repeat the process for the remaining pictures. Then direct students' attention to the next task. Say:

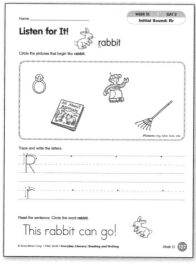

Day 2 activity

- *We are going to write uppercase* **R** *and lowercase* **r***. Start at the black dot on uppercase* **R***. Trace the line down. Go to the black dot again. Trace the line down around the curve. Go to the last line. Trace it down. Go to the next black dot. Write another uppercase* **R***.*

Guide students through writing two more uppercase **R**s. Then say:

- *Now let's write lowercase* **r***. Start at the black dot. Trace the line down. Go to the black dot again. Trace the curved line. Now write three more lowercase* **r***'s.*

- *Look at the sentence at the bottom of the page. It says* **This rabbit can go!** *Move your finger under each word as you read it with me:* **This rabbit can go!** *Circle the word* **rabbit***.*

SKILLS:
Concepts of Print
- Locate a printed word on a page
- Follow words from top to bottom and left to right
- Track print by pointing to written words when text is read aloud by self or others

Phonemic Awareness
- Segment the final phoneme of a spoken word

Phonics/Word Analysis
- Learn and apply letter-sound correspondences

Writing
- Print uppercase and lowercase letters
- Use spacing between letters and words when writing on a line

Reading and Writing Final *R*

Distribute the Day 3 activity and a writing tool. Say:

- *The spider in our story spun a web. Point to the spider at the top of the page. Say* **spider***. (spider) What is the* last *sound in* **spider***? (/r/) What letter stands for /r/? (R) Let's read the word* **spider** *together. Put your finger under the letter* **s***. Move your finger under the word as you read it with me:* **spider***.*

- *Now look at the pictures in the box. We're going to circle the pictures that* end *with /r/. Put your finger on the car. Say* **car***. (car) Does* **car** *end with /r/? (yes) Draw a circle around the car.*

Repeat the process for the remaining pictures. Then direct students' attention to the next task. Say:

Day 3 activity

- *Yesterday we followed the dots and the arrows to write uppercase and lowercase* **R***s. We are going to do it again today. Trace the uppercase* **R***. Then start at each dot and write an uppercase* **R***.*

- *Now trace the lowercase* **r***. Then start at each dot and write a lowercase* **r***.*

- *Look at the sentence at the bottom of the page. It says* **This spider can go!** *Move your finger under each word as you read it with me:* **This spider can go!** *Circle the word* **spider***.*

SKILLS:
Concepts of Print
• Locate a printed word on a page
• Follow words from top to bottom and left to right
• Track print by pointing to written words when text is read aloud by self or others

Phonemic Awareness
• Segment the initial phoneme of a spoken word

Phonics/Word Analysis
• Learn and apply letter-sound correspondences

Writing
• Print uppercase and lowercase letters
• Use spacing between letters and words when writing on a line

Initial and Final *R*

Reread the Day 1 story. Then guide a discussion about the story by saying:

The title of our story is "Rabbit Hops Away."

• *What animals were in the story?* (rabbit, spider, dog)

• *Whose garden were the animals in?* (Mrs. Ryan's)

• *Why do you think Mrs. Ryan did not like rabbits in her garden?* (They eat all the vegetables.)

Then distribute the Day 4 activity and a writing tool. Say:

• *Point to the first sentence. Move your finger under each word as we read together:* **This rabbit can go!** *Let's read it again:* **This rabbit can go!** *Draw a line to the picture that belongs with the sentence.*

• *Point to the next sentence. Move your finger under each word as we read together:* **This spider can go!** *Let's read it again:* **This spider can go!** *Draw a line to the picture that belongs with the sentence.*

• *Now look at the first box at the bottom of the page. We are listening for the word that begins with /r/. Let's name the pictures together:* **net, ring.** *Which word begins with /r/:* **net** *or* **ring**? (ring) *Circle the ring. The word* **ring** *begins with the letter* **r.**

• *Now look at the next box. We are going to circle the picture that ends with /r/. Let's say each picture name together:* **car, dress.** *Which word ends with /r/:* **car** *or* **dress**? (car) *Circle the car. The word* **car** *ends with the letter* **r.**

Day 4 activity

SKILLS:
Phonemic Awareness
• Identify the initial or final phoneme of a spoken word

Literary Response and Analysis
• Participate in a group response to a literary selection, identifying the characters, setting, and sequence of events

Comprehension
• Make connections using prior knowledge and real-life experiences

Circle Activity

Have students sit in a circle. Then review the Day 1 story and connect it to students' lives by asking:

• *Why do you think the spider said, "Eating vegetables is dangerous!"?*

• *Have you seen a spider in a web? Where?*

• *Have you ever seen a dog chase a rabbit?*

Have students practice distinguishing the initial and final **R** sound using the call-and-response activity below. Begin by having students sit cross-legged. Then teach them to respond to your call by patting their left knee when they say "first" and their right knee when they say "last." If necessary, place a sticker on students' left knee to help them remember right from left.

Recite the chant below as you alternate patting knees and clapping as you say each syllable.

Teacher: *Lis-ten, lis-ten, do you hear it?*
Let-ter **R.** *Let-ter* **R.**
Is it first, or is it last?
Tell me quick-ly, tell me fast: **rabbit!**

Students: *First!* (pat left knee)

Teacher: *Spider!*

Students: *Last!* (pat right knee)

Repeat the chant using the following words: *air, star, bear, car, ring, rake, robot.*

Rr

Rabbit Hops Away

Number the pictures in order.

Name _____

Listen for It!

 <u> </u>rabbit

Circle the pictures that begin like **rabbit**.

Pictures: *ring, robot, book, rake*

Trace and write the letters.

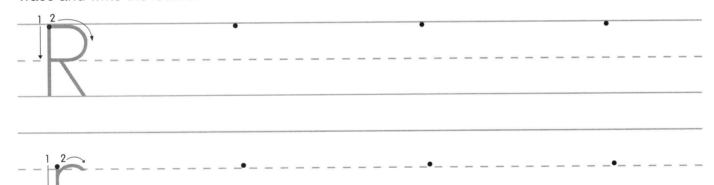

Read the sentence. Circle the word **rabbit**.

This rabbit can go!

Name _____

Listen for It!

 spider

Circle the pictures that <u>end</u> like **spider**.

Pictures: car, bear, goat, star

Trace and write the letters.

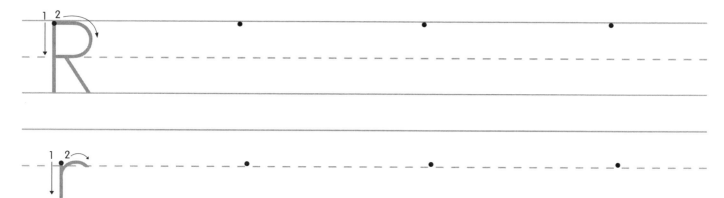

Read the sentence. Circle the word **spider**.

This spider can go!

Everyday Literacy: Reading and Writing • EMC 2418 • © Evan-Moor Corp.

Name _____

Read It!

Read the sentence.
Draw a line to the correct picture.

This rabbit can go!   ★

This spider can go!   ★

Circle the picture that begins with /r/.

r____

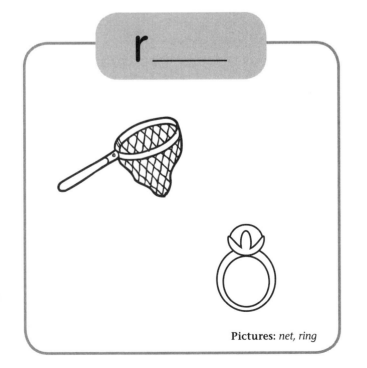

Pictures: *net, ring*

Circle the picture that <u>ends</u> with /r/.

____r

Pictures: *car, dress*

Name _____

Listen for the Sound of R r

Circle the pictures that <u>begin</u> with the same sound as **rabbit**.

Underline the pictures that <u>end</u> with the same sound as **spider**.

WEEK 15

Home–School Connection

To Parents

This week your child learned that **R** stands for the first sound in **rabbit** and the last sound in **spider**.

<u>r</u>abbit | spide<u>r</u>

Pictures: *rake, robot, car, bear, star, ring*

Trace and write the letters.

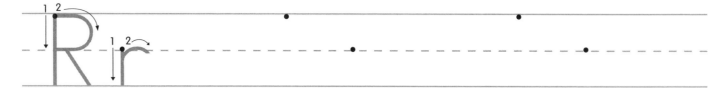

Everyday Literacy: Reading and Writing • EMC 2418 • © Evan-Moor Corp.

Concept

Initial and Final Sounds:

J, K, R

Review It

Vocabulary

Words with *j*, *k*, or *r* at the Beginning: June, kangaroo, rabbit

Words with *k* or *r* at the End: yak, spider

High-Frequency Words: a, are, can, go, this, you

Day 1

SKILLS:
Concepts of Print
- Identify uppercase and lowercase letters of the alphabet

Phonemic Awareness
- Isolate and identify the initial or final phoneme of a spoken word

Phonics/Word Analysis
- Recognize that individual letters have associated sounds

Writing
- Print uppercase and lowercase letters
- Use spacing between letters and words when writing on a line

I Know *Jj*, *Kk*, and *Rr*

Distribute the Day 1 activity and a writing tool to each student. Then say:

- *Point to June Bug dancing a jig. What is the first sound in* **jig***? (/j/) What letter stands for /j/? (J) Point to the uppercase* **J***. Trace it. Now point to the lowercase* **j***. Trace it. Now write two uppercase* **J***s and two lowercase* **j***'s on the line.*

- *Point to the kangaroo. What is the first sound in* **kangaroo***? (/k/) What letter stands for /k/? (K) Point to the uppercase* **K***. Trace it. Now point to the lowercase* **k***. Trace it. Now write two uppercase* **K***s and two lowercase* **k***'s on the line.*

Repeat the process for the remaining picture and letters. Then direct students' attention to the next task. Say:

- *Look at the uppercase alphabet at the bottom of the page. Let's name the letters together. (name aloud) Circle uppercase* **J***,* **K***, and* **R***.*

- *Look at the lowercase alphabet below. Let's name the letters together. (name aloud) Now circle lowercase* **j***,* **k***, and* **r***.*

Day 1 activity

Day 2

SKILLS:
Phonemic Awareness
- Identify the position of an isolated phoneme in a spoken word

Phonics/Word Analysis
- Learn and apply letter-sound correspondences
- Recognize that individual letters have associated sounds
- Read familiar CVC words and common sight words

Listening for *Jj*, *Kk*, and *Rr*

Distribute the Day 2 activity and a writing tool to each student. Then say:

- *We are going to listen for letter sounds. Point to the* **J** *row. What sound does* **J** *stand for? (/j/) Say* **jacket***. (jacket) Do you hear /j/ first or last in* **jacket***? (first) Fill in the first circle under the jacket. Say* **jeep***. (jeep) Do you hear /j/ first or last in* **jeep***? (first) Fill in the first circle under the jeep. Say* **jar***. (jar) Do you hear /j/ first or last in* **jar***? (first) Fill in the first circle under the jar.*

- *Point to the* **K** *row. What sound does* **K** *stand for? (/k/) Say* **kite***. (kite) Do you hear /k/ first or last in* **kite***? (first) Fill in the first circle under the kite. Say* **book***. (book) Do you hear /k/ first or last in* **book***? (last) Fill in the last circle. Say* **sock***. (sock) Do you hear /k/ first or last in* **sock***? (last) Fill in the last circle.*

Repeat the process for the remaining letter and pictures. Then direct students' attention to the next task. Say:

- *Point to the sentence at the bottom of the page. Move your finger under each word as you read it aloud. Now fill in the circle beside the matching picture.*

Day 2 activity

SKILLS:
Concepts of Print
• Understand that spoken words are represented in writing by specific sequences of letters

Phonemic Awareness
• Isolate and identify the initial or final sound of a spoken word

Phonics/Word Analysis
• Learn and apply letter-sound correspondences
• Recognize that individual letters have associated sounds
• Read familiar CVC words and common sight words

Writing
• Write the letters that match sounds in words

Writing Words with *J, K,* and *R*

Distribute the Day 3 activity and a writing tool to each student. Say:

Day 3 activity

- *Each box shows a picture and a word that is missing a letter. We are going to say each picture name and write the missing letter. Point to the first picture. It shows jam. Say **jam**. (jam) What is the first sound in **jam**? (/j/) Write the missing letter. Now move your finger under each letter as we read the word together: **jam**.*

- *Point to the picture in box 2. It shows a hook. Say **hook**. (hook) What is the last sound in **hook**? (/k/) Write the missing letter. Let's read the word together: **hook**.*

- *Point to the picture in box 3. What is it? (jet) What is the first sound in **jet**? (/j/) Write the missing letter. Let's read the word together: **jet**.*

- *Point to the picture in box 4. What is it? (car) What is the last sound in **car**? (/r/) Write the missing letter. Let's read the word together: **car**.*

- *Point to the picture in box 5. It shows a king. Say **king**. (king) What is the first sound in **king**? (/k/) Write the missing letter. Let's read the word together: **king**.*

- *Point to the picture in box 6. What is it? (rug) What is the first sound in **rug**? (/r/) Write the missing letter. Let's read the word together: **rug**.*

SKILLS:
Phonics/Word Analysis
• Learn and apply letter-sound correspondences
• Read familiar CVC words and common sight words

Comprehension
• Demonstrate comprehension of text read aloud by self or others

Reading Words with *J, K,* and *R*

Distribute the Day 4 activity and pencils or crayons. Then say:

Day 4 activity

- *Point to the first sentence. Move your finger under the words as we read together: **Can June Bug go?** Draw a line from this sentence to the picture it matches.*

- *Point to sentence 2. Move your finger under the words as we read together: **Can this kangaroo go?** Draw a line from the sentence to the picture it matches.*

- *Point to sentence 3. Let's read it together: **Can this yak go?** Draw a line from the sentence to the picture it matches.*

- *Point to sentence 4. Let's read it together: **Can this rabbit go?** Draw a line from the sentence to the picture it matches.*

- *Point to sentence 5. Let's read it together: **Can this spider go?** Draw a line from the sentence to the picture it matches.*

- *Point to the last sentence on the page. Write a word to complete the sentence. Then draw a picture that matches what you wrote.*

Day 5

SKILLS:

Phonemic Awareness

• Isolate and identify the initial or final phoneme of a spoken word

Phonics/Word Analysis

• Learn and apply letter-sound correspondences

• Recognize that individual letters have associated sounds

Home–School Connection p. 138
Spanish version available (see p. 2)

Phonics Review Game

Play the following game to review the initial and final consonant sounds that students have learned this week.

Materials: 6 large index cards or 3 sheets of construction paper cut in half

Preparation: Write the letter **j** on two cards, the letter **k** on two cards, and the letter **r** on two cards. Divide the cards into two sets that contain one of each letter. Display one set of cards on each end of the board.

How to Play: Divide students into two teams. Have each team line up facing the board. Explain to students that you will say a word and that they should listen for the beginning sound. After you say the word, the first player in each line races up to the board, chooses the correct letter card, faces his or her team, and says the letter name aloud. Each correct answer is worth one point. The two players then return the cards to the ledge and go to the end of the line. Repeat the process until you have called all of the words in the chart below. The team with the most points wins. Play the game again, and have students listen for ending sounds.

Beginning Sounds:	Ending Sounds:
J: jet, jam, June, jacket, jeep **K:** kite, king, kick, kangaroo **R:** ring, rake, rabbit, rug	**K:** hook, book, sock, yak **R:** car, deer, star, jar, spider

Write It!

Trace then write each letter.

Find uppercase **J**, **K**, and **R**. Circle them.

A	B	C	D	E	F	G	H	I	J	K	L	M
N	O	P	Q	R	S	T	U	V	W	X	Y	Z

Find lowercase **j**, **k**, and **r**. Circle them.

a	b	c	d	e	f	g	h	i	j	k	l	m
n	o	p	q	r	s	t	u	v	w	x	y	z

Name _____

Listen for It!

Where do you hear the letter sound?
Fill in the circle to show **first** or **last**.

J j

K k

R r

Read the sentence.
Fill in the circle next to the correct picture.

You are a yak.

Spell It!

Say each picture name.
Write the missing letter.

j k r

1

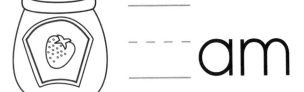
_ _ am

2

hoo _ _

3

_ _ et

4

ca _ _

5

_ _ ing

6

_ _ ug

Everyday Literacy: Reading and Writing • EMC 2418 • © Evan-Moor Corp.

Read It!

Read the sentence.
Draw a line to the correct picture.

1 Can June Bug go?

2 Can this kangaroo go?

3 Can this yak go?

4 Can this rabbit go?

5 Can this spider go?

Complete the sentence.
Draw a picture to match.

Can this _____ go?

Name _____

Beginning and Ending

Jj Kk Rr

WEEK 16

Home–School Connection

To Parents
This week your child reviewed beginning and ending sounds for the letters **J**, **K**, and **R**.

Name each picture. Draw a line to show what letter sound you hear at the **beginning**.

 •

 •

 •

j

r

k

Pictures: *kite, jet, ring*

Name each picture. Draw a line to show what letter sound you hear at the **end**.

 •

 •

r

k

Pictures: *book, star*

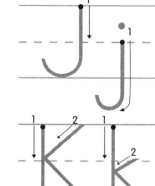

Everyday Literacy: Reading and Writing • EMC 2418 • © Evan-Moor Corp.

WEEK 17
Hh

If I Had a Horse

Concept: H stands for the first sound in **horse**.
High-Frequency Words: big, is, little, my, this

Learning About the Letter *Hh*

Distribute the Day 1 activity page. Say: *This week's letter is* **H***. Find* **H** *at the top of the page. Point to the uppercase* **H***. Now point to the lowercase* **h***. The letter* **H** *stands for this sound:* /h/. *Say* /h/. (/h/) *It is the first sound you hear in* **horse***. Say* **horse***.* (horse) *What sound does the letter* **H** *stand for?* (/h/)

Listening to the Story

To prepare students to listen to the story, say: *I am going to read you a story called "If I Had a Horse." Look at the picture. What do you think happens in the story?* (students respond) *Listen for the* /h/ *sound as I read the story.*

Every night when I go to bed, I lie awake and think about what it would be like to have a **horse** *for a pet. I live in an apartment building in the city, where horses aren't allowed. But when I'm in bed at night, I imagine that I live in a big* **house** *in the country and my horse lives outside in the barn. I imagine all the things I would do to take care of my horse. First, I would pet it every morning before school. Then, I would ride it every day after school. Next, I would brush its long tail* **hair***. Before I put my horse to bed at night, I would feed it* **hay***. That's* **how** *I imagine it would be to take care of a horse.*

Thinking About the Story

Distribute crayons or markers. Guide students in answering questions about the story. Say:

Day 1 picture

• *Look at the big picture. What kind of pet does the girl like to imagine she has?* (a horse) *Do you hear* /h/ *in* **horse***?* (yes) *Use red to circle one of the horses in the picture.*

• *Where does the girl live?* (an apartment in the city) *Where does she imagine she lives?* (a house in the country) *Do you hear* /h/ *in* **house***?* (yes)

• *Look at the little pictures at the bottom of the page. Number the pictures to show what the girl imagined she would do to take care of her horse. What would she do first?* (pet her horse every morning) *Write* **1** *under the picture of her petting her horse.*

• *What would she do next?* (brush its tail) *Write* **2** *under the picture.*

• *What would she do before she puts her horse to bed at night?* (feed it hay) *Write* **3** *under the picture.*

Day 2

SKILLS:

Concepts of Print
- Locate a printed word on a page
- Follow words from top to bottom and left to right
- Track print by pointing to written words when text is read aloud by self or others

Phonemic Awareness
- Segment the initial phoneme of a spoken word

Phonics/Word Analysis
- Learn and apply letter-sound correspondences

Writing
- Print uppercase and lowercase letters
- Use spacing between letters and words when writing on a line

Reading and Writing Initial *H*

Distribute the Day 2 activity and a writing tool. Say:

Day 2 activity

- *Yesterday we read a story about a girl who likes horses. Point to the horse at the top of the page. Say* **horse**. *(horse) What is the first sound in* **horse**? *(/h/) What letter stands for* **/h/**? *(H) Let's read the word* **horse** *together. Put your finger under the letter* **h**. *Move your finger under the word as you read it with me:* **horse**.

- *Now look at the pictures in the box. We're going to circle the pictures that begin with* **/h/**. *Point to the hand. Say* **hand**. *(hand) Does* **hand** *begin with* **/h/**? *(yes) Draw a circle around the hand.*

Repeat the process for the remaining pictures. Then direct students' attention to the next task. Say:

- *We are going to write uppercase* **H** *and lowercase* **h**. *Start at the black dot on uppercase* **H**. *Trace the line down. Go to the line beside the number 2. Trace the line down. Go to the last line and follow it across. Go to the next black dot. Write another uppercase* **H**.

Guide students through writing two more uppercase Hs. Then say:

- *Now let's write lowercase* **h**. *Start at the black dot. Trace the line down. Go to the line below the number 2. Follow the line around and down. Now write three more lowercase* **h**'s.

- *Look at the sentence at the bottom of the page. It says* **My horse is big**. *Move your finger under each word as you read it with me:* **My horse is big**. *Circle the word* **horse**.

Day 3

SKILLS:

Concepts of Print
- Locate a printed word on a page
- Follow words from top to bottom and left to right
- Track print by pointing to written words when text is read aloud by self or others

Phonemic Awareness
- Recognize a phoneme in a spoken word

Comprehension
- Answer questions about text read aloud

Writing
- Print uppercase and lowercase letters
- Use spacing between letters and words when writing on a line

Listening for Initial *H*

Reread the Day 1 story. Then guide a discussion about the story by saying:

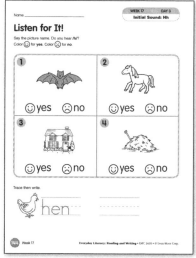

Day 3 activity

Our story was about a girl who imagined she had a horse for a pet. Where did the girl live? Where did she imagine she lived? (an apartment in the city; a big house in the country)

Distribute the Day 3 activity and a writing tool. Say:

- *This week we are learning about the letter* **H**. *What sound does the letter* **H** *stand for? (/h/)*

- *Point to the bat in box 1. Say* **bat**. *(bat) Do you hear* **/h/** *in* **bat**? *(no) Color the happy face for* **yes** *or the sad face for* **no**.

- *Point to the horse. Say* **horse**. *(horse) Do you hear* **/h/** *in* **horse**? *(yes) Color the happy face for* **yes** *or the sad face for* **no**.

- *Point to the house. Say* **house**. *(house) Do you hear* **/h/** *in* **house**? *(yes) Color the happy face for* **yes** *or the sad face for* **no**.

- *Point to the hay. Say* **hay**. *(hay) Do you hear* **/h/** *in* **hay**? *(yes) Color the happy face for* **yes** *or the sad face for* **no**.

- *Now point to the hen. What is the first sound in* **hen**? *(/h/) Move your finger under the word as we read it together:* **hen**. *Trace the word* **hen** *and then write it on the next line.*

Day 4

SKILLS:

Phonemic Awareness
- Isolate and identify the initial phoneme of a spoken word

Alphabet/Word Recognition
- Recognize that individual letters have associated sounds

Concepts of Print
- Locate a printed word on a page

Writing
- Use spacing between letters and words when writing on a line

Reading and Writing with Initial *H*

Reread the Day 1 story. Then say:

The title of this week's story is "If I Had a Horse."

- *When does the girl think about having a horse?* (every night when she's in bed)
- *What does she imagine she feeds her horse?* (hay)

Then distribute the Day 4 activity and a writing tool. Say:

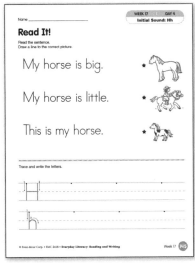

Day 4 activity

- *Point to the first sentence. Move your finger under each word as we read together:* **My horse is big.** *Let's read it again:* **My horse is big.** *Which picture belongs with this sentence?* (big horse) *Draw a line to the big horse.*

- *Point to the next sentence. Move your finger under each word as we read together:* **My horse is little.** *Let's read it again:* **My horse is little.** *Which picture belongs with this sentence?* (the little horse) *Draw a line to the little horse.*

- *Point to the last sentence. Move your finger under each word as we read together:* **This is my horse.** *Let's read it again:* **This is my horse.** *Which picture belongs with this sentence?* (the girl riding a horse) *Draw a line to the girl riding a horse.*

- *Now we are going to write uppercase* **H** *and lowercase* **h.** *Let's start with uppercase* **H.** *Start at the black dot. Trace the uppercase* **H.** *Then write three more uppercase* **H**s.

- *Now let's write lowercase* **h.** *Start at the black dot. Trace the lowercase* **h.** *Now write three more lowercase* **h**'s.

Day 5

SKILLS:

Phonemic Awareness
- Identify the initial phoneme of a spoken word

Literary Response and Analysis
- Participate in a group response to a literary selection, identifying the characters, setting, and sequence of events

Comprehension
- Make connections using prior knowledge and real-life experiences

Home–School Connection p. 146
Spanish version available (see p. 2)

Circle Activity

Have students sit in a circle. Then review the Day 1 story and connect it to students' lives by asking:

- *What did the girl imagine she would do to take care of her pet?*
- *Do you live in the city or country? What kind of pet do you like to imagine having?*

Have students practice distinguishing the initial **H** sound using the call-and-response activity below. Begin by having students sit cross-legged. Then teach them to respond to your call by patting their left knee when they say "yes" and their right knee when they say "no." If necessary, place a sticker on students' left knee to help them remember right from left.

Recite the chant below as you alternate patting knees and clapping as you say each syllable.

Teacher: *Lis-ten, lis-ten, do you hear it?*
Let-ter **H.** *Let-ter* **H.** *It says* /h/. *It says* /h/.
Do you hear it? Yes or no?
Lis-ten: **Horse!**

Students: *Yes!* (pat left knee)

Teacher: *Cat!*

Students: *No!* (pat right knee)

Repeat the chant using the following words: *hay, hat, hook, hair, hand.*

Name _____

Hh

If I Had a Horse

Number the pictures in order.

Everyday Literacy: Reading and Writing • EMC 2418 • © Evan-Moor Corp.

Name _____

Listen for It!

 <u>h</u>orse

Circle the pictures that begin like **horse**.

Pictures: *hand, house, hen, cat*

Trace and write the letters.

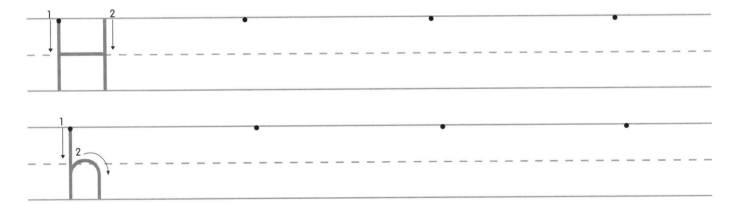

Read the sentence. Circle the word **horse**.

My horse is big.

Listen for It!

Say the picture name. Do you hear **/h/**?
Color 🙂 for **yes**. Color ☹ for **no**.

1
🙂 yes   ☹ no

2
🙂 yes   ☹ no

3
🙂 yes   ☹ no

4
🙂 yes   ☹ no

Trace then write.

hen

Everyday Literacy: Reading and Writing • EMC 2418 • © Evan-Moor Corp.

Name _____

Read It!

Read the sentence.
Draw a line to the correct picture.

My horse is big.

My horse is little.

This is my horse.

Trace and write the letters.

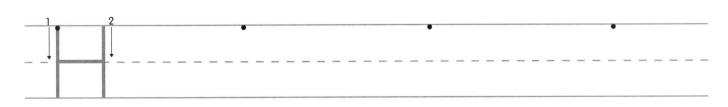

Everyday Literacy: Reading and Writing

Name _____

Listen for the Sound of **Hh**

Circle the pictures that begin with the same sound as **horse**.

WEEK 17

Home–School Connection

To Parents

This week your child learned that **H** stands for the first sound in **horse**.

<u>h</u>orse

Pictures: *hand, kangaroo, house, hen, hay*

Trace and write the letters.

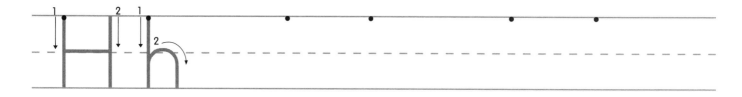

Pinky Pig

Concept: **P** stands for the first sound in **pig** and the last sound in **sheep**.
High-Frequency Words: a, are, you

SKILLS:
Concepts of Print

• Identify uppercase and lowercase letters of the alphabet

Phonemic Awareness

• Recognize a phoneme in a spoken word

Phonics/Word Analysis

• Learn and apply letter-sound correspondences

• Produce the sound a consonant letter makes in isolation

Literary Response and Analysis

• Participate in a group response to a literary selection, identifying the characters, setting, and sequence of events

• Make predictions about text content using pictures, background knowledge, and text features

Comprehension

• Answer questions about text read aloud

• Respond to *who, what, where, why, how* questions about text read aloud

Learning About the Letter *Pp*

Distribute the Day 1 activity page. Say: *This week's letter is* **P**. *Find* **P** *at the top of the page. Point to the uppercase* **P**. *Now point to the lowercase* **p**. *The letter* **P** *stands for this sound:* **/p/**. *Say* **/p/**. (/p/) *It is the first sound you hear in* **pig**. *Say* **pig**. (pig) *It is the* last *sound you hear in* **sheep**. *Say* **sheep**. (sheep) *What sound does the letter* **P** *stand for?* (/p/)

Listening to the Story

To prepare students to listen to the story, say: *I am going to read you a story. The title is "Pinky Pig." Look at the picture. What do you think happens in the story?* (students respond) *Listen for the* **/p/** *sound as I read the story.*

---

    *Pinky Pig is a hard worker. He collects apples and gives them to Shelly **Sheep**. Pinky shakes the apple tree until the apples fall into a **pile**. Then he picks them **up** and puts them into a **pail**. All the animals look at each other and say, "That Pinky Pig is such a hard worker. But why does he only **pick** apples? The **peaches** and **pears** are ready, too. It's a mystery." Shelly Sheep knew why Pinky worked so hard collecting apples for her. There was only one thing on Pinky's mind as he worked all day. It rhymes with "sky." Can you guess what it is? You're right! Pinky loves Shelly's delicious apple **pie**!*

Thinking About the Story

Distribute crayons or markers. Guide students in answering questions about the story. Say:

Day 1 picture

• *Look at the big picture. Who is this story mostly about?* (Pinky Pig) *Do you hear* **/p/** *in* **Pinky**? (yes) *Make a pink dot on Pinky.*

• *What fruit does Pinky collect?* (apples) *Make a red dot on the apples. Who does Pinky give the apples to?* (Shelly Sheep) *Do you hear* **/p/** *in* **sheep**? (yes)

• *Look at the little pictures at the bottom of the page. Let's number the pictures to show what Pinky did in the story. What did Pinky do first?* (shook the apple tree) *Write* **1** *under the picture.*

• *What did Pinky do next?* (put the apples into a pail) *Write* **2** *under the picture.*

• *What happens to the apples at the end of the story?* (Shelly bakes them in an apple pie.) *Write* **3** *under the picture.*

Day 2

SKILLS:

Concepts of Print

- Locate a printed word on a page
- Follow words from top to bottom and left to right
- Track print by pointing to written words when text is read aloud by self or others

Phonemic Awareness

- Segment the initial phoneme of a spoken word

Phonics/Word Analysis

- Learn and apply letter-sound correspondences

Writing

- Print uppercase and lowercase letters
- Use spacing between letters and words when writing on a line

Reading and Writing Initial *P*

Distribute the Day 2 activity and a writing tool. Say:

- *Yesterday we read a story about a pig who loves apple pie. Point to the pig. Say* **pig**. *(pig) What is the first sound in* **pig**? *(/p/) What letter stands for* **/p/**? *(P) Let's read the word* **pig** *together. Put your finger under the letter* **p**. *Move your finger under the word as you read it with me:* **pig**.

- *Now look at the pictures in the box. We're going to circle the pictures that* begin *with* **/p/**. *Point to the pear. Say* **pear**. *(pear) Does* **pear** *begin with* **/p/**? *(yes) Draw a circle around the pear.*

Repeat the process for the remaining pictures. Then direct students' attention to the next task. Say:

- *We are going to write uppercase* **P** *and lowercase* **p**. *Start at the black dot on uppercase* **P**. *Trace the line down. Go to the black dot again. Trace the line down around the curve. Go to the next black dot. Write another uppercase* **P**.

Guide students through writing two more uppercase Ps. Then say:

- *Now let's write lowercase* **p**. *Start at the black dot. Trace the line down. Go to the black dot again. Trace the line down around the curve. Now write three more lowercase* **p**'s.

- *Look at the sentence at the bottom of the page. It says* **You are a pig**. *Move your finger under each word as you read it with me:* **You are a pig**. *Circle the word* **pig**.

Day 2 activity

Day 3

SKILLS:

Concepts of Print

- Locate a printed word on a page
- Follow words from top to bottom and left to right
- Track print by pointing to written words when text is read aloud by self or others

Phonemic Awareness

- Segment the final phoneme of a spoken word

Phonics/Word Analysis

- Learn and apply letter-sound correspondences

Writing

- Print uppercase and lowercase letters
- Use spacing between letters and words when writing on a line

Reading and Writing Final *P*

Distribute the Day 3 activity and a writing tool. Say:

- *In our story this week, Shelly Sheep bakes Pinky Pig apple pies. Point to the sheep. Say* **sheep**. *(sheep) What is the* last *sound in* **sheep**? *(/p/) What letter stands for* **/p/**? *(P) Let's read the word* **sheep** *together. Put your finger under the letter* **s**. *Move your finger under the word as you read it with me:* **sheep**.

- *Now look at the pictures in the box. We're going to circle the pictures that* end *with* **/p/**. *Put your finger on the cap. Say* **cap**. *(cap) Does* **cap** *end with* **/p/**? *(yes) Draw a circle around the cap.*

Repeat the process for the remaining pictures. Then direct students' attention to the next task. Say:

- *Yesterday we followed the dots and the arrows to write uppercase and lowercase* **P**s. *We are going to do it again today. Trace the uppercase* **P**. *Then start at each dot and write an uppercase* **P**.

- *Now trace the lowercase* **p**. *Then start at each dot and write a lowercase* **p**.

- *Look at the sentence at the bottom of the page. It says* **You are a sheep**. *Move your finger under each word as you read it with me:* **You are a sheep**. *Circle the word* **sheep**.

Day 3 activity

Day 4

SKILLS:

Concepts of Print
- Locate a printed word on a page

Phonemic Awareness
- Identify the initial or final phoneme of a spoken word

Phonics/Word Recognition
- Recognize that individual letters have associated sounds

Literary Response and Analysis
- Participate in a group response to a literary selection, identifying the characters, setting, and sequence of events

Comprehension
- Answer questions about text read aloud
- Respond to *who, what, where, why, how* questions about text read aloud

Initial and Final *P*

Reread the Day 1 story. Then guide a discussion about the story by saying:

Our story was about Pinky Pig and Shelly Sheep.
- *What does Pinky do all day?* (collect apples)
- *Who does he give them to?* (Shelly Sheep)
- *What does she do with them?* (puts them in a pie)

Then distribute the Day 4 activity and a writing tool. Say:

- *Point to the first sentence. Move your finger under each word as we read together:* **You are a pig.** *Let's read it again:* **You are a pig.** *Which picture belongs with this sentence?* (the pig) *Draw a line to the picture that belongs with the sentence.*

- *Point to the next sentence. Move your finger under each word as we read together:* **You are a sheep.** *Let's read it again:* **You are a sheep.** *Which picture belongs with this sentence?* (the sheep) *Draw a line to the picture that belongs with the sentence.*

- *Now look at the first box at the bottom of the page. We are listening for the word that* <u>begins</u> *with* **/p/**. *Let's name the pictures together:* **pie, sun.** *Which word begins with* **/p/**: **pie** *or* **sun**? (pie) *Circle the pie. The word* **pie** *begins with the letter* **p**.

- *Now look at the next box. We are going to circle the picture that* <u>ends</u> *with* **/p/**. *Let's say each picture name together:* **house, map.** *Which word ends with* **/p/**: **house** *or* **map**? (map) *Circle the map. The word* **map** *ends with the letter* **p**.

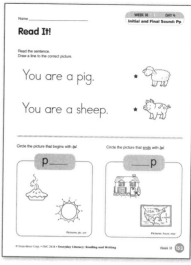

Day 4 activity

Day 5

SKILLS:

Phonemic Awareness
- Identify the initial or final phoneme of a spoken word

Literary Response and Analysis
- Participate in a group response to a literary selection, identifying the characters, setting, and sequence of events

Comprehension
- Make connections using prior knowledge and real-life experiences

Home–School Connection p. 154
Spanish version available (see p. 2)

Circle Activity

Have students sit in a circle. Then review the Day 1 story and connect it to students' lives by asking:

- *What other fruit was ready for Pinky to collect?*
- *Have you ever picked fruit from a tree? What kind of fruit was it? Did you eat it?*

Have students practice distinguishing initial and final **P** using the call-and-response activity below. Begin by having students sit cross-legged. Then teach them to respond to your call by patting their left knee when they say "first" and their right knee when they say "last." If necessary, place a sticker on students' left knee to help them remember right from left.

Recite the chant below as you alternate patting knees and clapping as you say each syllable.

Teacher: *Lis-ten, lis-ten, do you hear it?*
Let-ter **P**. *Let-ter* **P**.
Is it first, or is it last?
Tell me quick-ly, tell me fast: **pig**!

Students: *First!* (pat left knee)

Teacher: ***Sheep***!

Students: *Last!* (pat right knee)

Repeat the chant using the following words: *pail, peaches, pears, keep, up, map.*

Pp

Pinky Pig

Number the pictures in order.

Everyday Literacy: Reading and Writing • EMC 2418 • © Evan-Moor Corp.

Name _____

Listen for It!

 <u>p</u>ig

Circle the pictures that begin like **pig**.

Pictures: *pear, pie, lion, pencil*

Trace and write the letters.

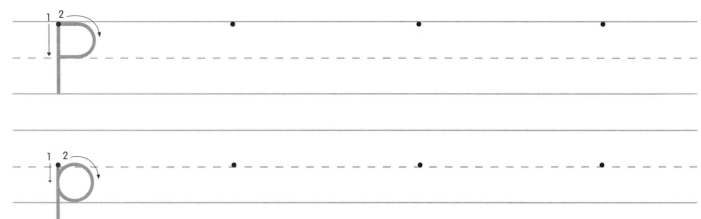

Read the sentence. Circle the word **pig**.

You are a pig.

Everyday Literacy: Reading and Writing Week 18 **151**

Name _____

Listen for It!

 sheep

Circle the pictures that <u>end</u> like **sheep**.

Pictures: *cap, key, map, cup*

Trace and write the letters.

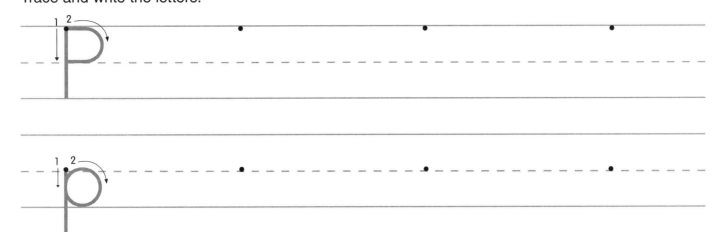

Read the sentence. Circle the word **sheep**.

You are a sheep.

Read It!

Read the sentence.
Draw a line to the correct picture.

You are a pig.

★

You are a sheep.

★

Circle the picture that begins with /p/.

p_____

Pictures: *pie, sun*

Circle the picture that <u>ends</u> with /p/.

_____p

Pictures: *house, map*

Name _____

Listen for the Sound of P p

Circle the pictures that <u>begin</u> with the same sound as **pig**.

Underline the pictures that <u>end</u> with the same sound as **sheep**.

WEEK 18
Home–School Connection

To Parents

This week your child learned that **P** stands for the first sound in **pig** and the last sound in **sheep**.

pi<u>g</u>   shee<u>p</u>

Pictures: *cup, pencil, pie, map, cap, pear*

Trace and write the letters.

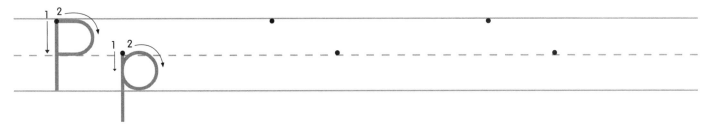

Everyday Literacy: Reading and Writing • EMC 2418 • © Evan-Moor Corp.

Baby Walrus

Concept: **W** stands for the first sound in **walrus**.
High-Frequency Words: a, big, is, little, not, that

Day 1

SKILLS:

Concepts of Print

• Identify uppercase and lowercase letters of the alphabet

Phonemic Awareness

• Recognize a phoneme in a spoken word

Phonics/Word Analysis

• Learn and apply letter-sound correspondences

• Produce the sound a consonant letter makes in isolation

Literary Response and Analysis

• Participate in a group response to a literary selection, identifying the characters, setting, and sequence of events

• Make predictions about text content using pictures, background knowledge, and text features

Comprehension

• Answer questions about text read aloud

• Respond to *who, what, where, why, how* questions about text read aloud

Learning About the Letter *Ww*

Distribute the Day 1 activity page. Say: *This week's letter is **W**. Find **W** at the top of the page. Point to the uppercase **W**. Now point to the lowercase **w**. The letter **W** stands for this sound: /w/. Say /w/. (/w/) It is the first sound you hear in **walrus**. Say **walrus**. (walrus) What sound does the letter **W** stand for? (/w/)*

Listening to the Story

To prepare students to listen to the story, say: *I am going to read you a story. The title is "Baby Walrus." Look at the picture. What do you think happens in the story? (students respond) Listen for the /w/ sound as I read the story.*

---

*I am a baby **walrus**. Even though I am just a pup, I already know how to swim. I live in the icy ocean **with** my mom. Our favorite thing to do is float on a big chunk of ice. I like to climb onto my mom's back as **we** drift along together on the ice floe. I feel safe there. She feeds me and hugs me. But after we are done resting, my mom and I have **work** to do. My mom is teaching me how to be a grown-up walrus. First, she teaches me how to **watch** for polar bears. Next, she shows me how she uses her two huge teeth, which are called tusks, to pull herself up out of the **water**. Last, she teaches me how to lie down and rest on an ice floe—that is my favorite lesson of all!*

Thinking About the Story

Distribute crayons or markers. Guide students in answering questions about the story. Say:

• *What is the title of the story?* (Baby Walrus)

• *Look at the big picture. Who is telling the story?* (the baby walrus) *Do you hear /w/ in **walrus**?* (yes) *Another name for a baby walrus is **pup**. Make a brown dot on the pup.*

• *What are the mother walrus's two huge teeth called?* (tusks) *Circle the mother walrus's tusks.*

• *Look at the pictures at the bottom of the page. Which picture shows what the pup learned first?* (watching for polar bears) *Write **1** under the picture.*

• *Which picture shows what the pup learned next?* (using tusks to get out of the water) *Write **2** under the picture.*

• *Which picture shows what the pup learned last?* (resting on an ice floe) *Write **3** under the picture.*

Day 1 picture

SKILLS:
Concepts of Print
- Locate a printed word on a page
- Follow words from top to bottom and left to right
- Track print by pointing to written words when text is read aloud by self or others

Phonemic Awareness
- Segment the initial phoneme of a spoken word

Phonics/Word Analysis
- Learn and apply letter-sound correspondences

Writing
- Print uppercase and lowercase letters
- Use spacing between letters and words when writing on a line

Reading and Writing Initial *W*

Distribute the Day 2 activity and a writing tool. Say:

- *Yesterday we read a story about a baby walrus and a mother walrus. Point to the walrus at the top of the page. Say **walrus**. (walrus) What is the first sound in **walrus**? (/w/) What letter stands for /w/? (W) Let's read the word **walrus** together. Put your finger under the letter **w**. Move your finger under the word as you read it with me: **walrus**.*

- *Now look at the pictures in the box. We're going to circle the pictures that begin with /w/. Point to the window. Say **window**. (window) Does **window** begin with /w/? (yes) Draw a circle around the window.*

Repeat the process for the remaining pictures. Then direct students' attention to the next task. Say:

- *We are going to write uppercase **W** and lowercase **w**. Start at the black dot on uppercase **W**. Trace the line down and follow it up and down and up again. Go to the next black dot. Write another uppercase **W**.*

Guide students through writing two more uppercase *W*s. Then say:

- *Now let's write lowercase **w**. Start at the black dot. Trace the line down and follow it up and down and up again. Write three more lowercase **w**'s.*

- *Look at the sentence at the bottom of the page. It says **That is a big walrus**. Move your finger under each word as you read it with me: **That is a big walrus**. Circle the word **walrus**.*

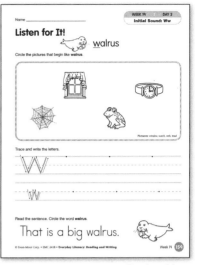

Day 2 activity

SKILLS:
Concepts of Print
- Locate a printed word on a page
- Follow words from top to bottom and left to right
- Track print by pointing to written words when text is read aloud by self or others

Phonemic Awareness
- Recognize a phoneme in a spoken word

Comprehension
- Respond to *who, what, where, why, how* questions about text read aloud

Writing
- Print uppercase and lowercase letters
- Use spacing between letters and words when writing on a line

Listening for Initial *W*

Reread the Day 1 story. Then guide a discussion about the story by saying:

Our story was about a walrus pup who was learning how to be a grown-up walrus. Who taught the walrus pup how to be a grown-up? (the mom walrus)

Distribute the Day 3 activity and a writing tool. Say:

- *This week we are learning about the letter **W**. What sound does the letter **W** stand for? (/w/)*

- *Point to the wagon in box 1. Say **wagon**. (wagon) Do you hear /w/ in **wagon**? (yes) Color the happy face for **yes** or the sad face for **no**.*

- *Point to the worm. Say **worm**. (worm) Do you hear /w/ in **worm**? (yes) Color the happy face for **yes** or the sad face for **no**.*

- *Point to the monkey. Say **monkey**. (monkey) Do you hear /w/ in **monkey**? (no) Color the happy face for **yes** or the sad face for **no**.*

- *Point to the water. Say **water**. (water) Do you hear /w/ in **water**? (yes) Color the happy face for **yes** or the sad face for **no**.*

- *Now point to the walrus from this week's story. Point to the word **walrus**. Move your finger under the word as we read it together: **walrus**. Trace the word **walrus** and then write it on the next line.*

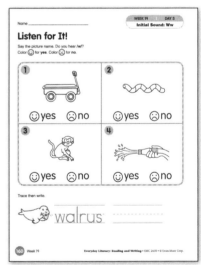

Day 3 activity

SKILLS:
Concepts of Print
• Locate a printed word on a page

Phonemic Awareness
• Identify the initial phoneme of a spoken word

Phonics/Word Recognition
• Recognize that individual letters have associated sounds

Literary Response and Analysis
• Participate in a group response to a literary selection, identifying the characters, setting, and sequence of events

Comprehension
• Answer questions about text read aloud
• Respond to *who, what, where, why, how* questions about text read aloud

Reading and Writing with Initial *W*

Reread the Day 1 story. Then guide a discussion about the story by saying:

Our story this week was about walruses.

• *Where do the walruses live?* (in the icy ocean)

• *What are tusks?* (teeth) *What can a walrus use its tusks to do?* (pull itself out of the water)

Then distribute the Day 4 activity and a writing tool. Say:

• *Point to the first sentence. Move your finger under each word as we read together:* **That is a big walrus**. *Let's read it again:* **That is a big walrus**. *Which picture belongs with this sentence?* (larger walrus) *Draw a line to the big walrus.*

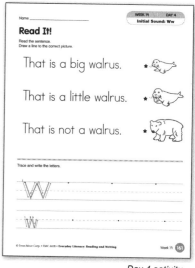

Day 4 activity

• *Point to the next sentence. Move your finger under each word as we read together:* **That is a little walrus**. *Let's read it again:* **That is a little walrus**. *Which picture belongs with this sentence?* (the little walrus) *Draw a line to the little walrus.*

• *Point to the last sentence. Move your finger under each word as we read together:* **That is not a walrus**. *Let's read it again:* **That is not a walrus**. *Which picture belongs with this sentence?* (the polar bear) *Draw a line to the polar bear.*

• *Now we are going to write uppercase* **W** *and lowercase* **w**. *Let's start with uppercase* **W**. *Trace the line down and follow it up and down and up again. Write three more uppercase* **W**s.

• *Now let's write lowercase* **w**. *Start at the black dot. Trace the line down and follow it up and down and up again. Write three more lowercase* **w**'s.

Day 5

SKILLS:
Phonemic Awareness
• Identify the initial phoneme of a spoken word

Literary Response and Analysis
• Participate in a group response to a literary selection, identifying the characters, setting, and sequence of events

Comprehension
• Make connections using prior knowledge and real-life experiences

Circle Activity

Have students sit in a circle. Then review the Day 1 story and connect it to students' lives by asking:

• *Pretend that you could float on a chunk of ice in the ocean. What might you see around you?*

Have students practice distinguishing the initial **W** sound using the call-and-response activity below. Begin by having students sit cross-legged. Then teach them to respond to your call by patting their left knee when they say "yes" and their right knee when they say "no." If necessary, place a sticker on students' left knee to help them remember right from left.

Recite the chant below as you alternate patting knees and clapping as you say each syllable.

Teacher: *Lis-ten, lis-ten, do you hear it?*
Let-ter **W**. *Let-ter* **W**. *It says* /w/. *It says* /w/.
Do you hear it? Yes or no?
Lis-ten: **Walrus**!

Students: *Yes!* (pat left knee)

Teacher: *Tree!*

Students: *No!* (pat right knee)

Repeat the chant using the following words: *window, watch, water, wings, wagon, web, well, winter.*

Name _____

Ww

Baby Walrus

Number the pictures in order.

Everyday Literacy: Reading and Writing • EMC 2418 • © Evan-Moor Corp.

Name _____

Listen for It!

 <u>w</u>alrus

Circle the pictures that begin like **walrus**.

Pictures: *window, watch, web, toad*

Trace and write the letters.

Read the sentence. Circle the word **walrus**.

That is a big walrus.

Listen for It!

Say the picture name. Do you hear /w/?
Color 😊 for **yes**. Color ☹ for **no**.

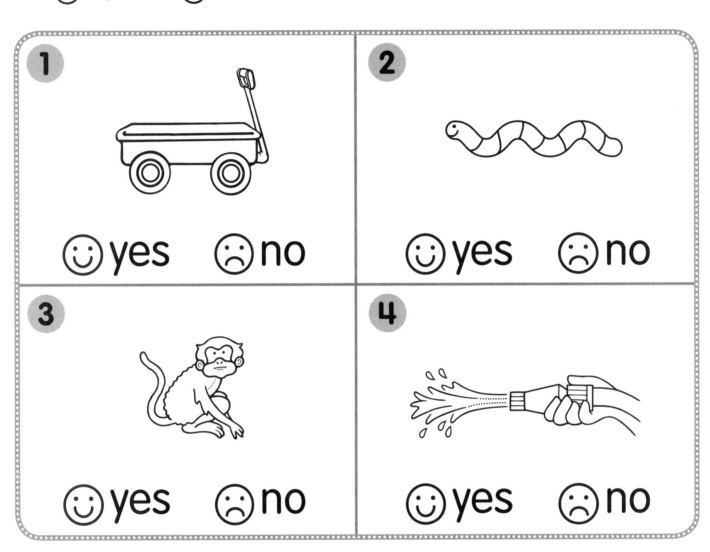

1. 😊 yes   ☹ no

2. 😊 yes   ☹ no

3. 😊 yes   ☹ no

4. 😊 yes   ☹ no

Trace then write.

walrus _____

Name _____

Read It!

Read the sentence.
Draw a line to the correct picture.

That is a big walrus.   ★

That is a little walrus.   ★

That is not a walrus.   ★

Trace and write the letters.

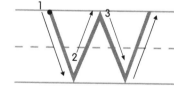

Name _____

Listen for the Sound of **Ww**

WEEK 19

Home–School Connection

To Parents

This week your child learned that **W** stands for the first sound in **walrus**.

Circle the pictures that begin with the same sound as **walrus**.

<u>w</u>alrus

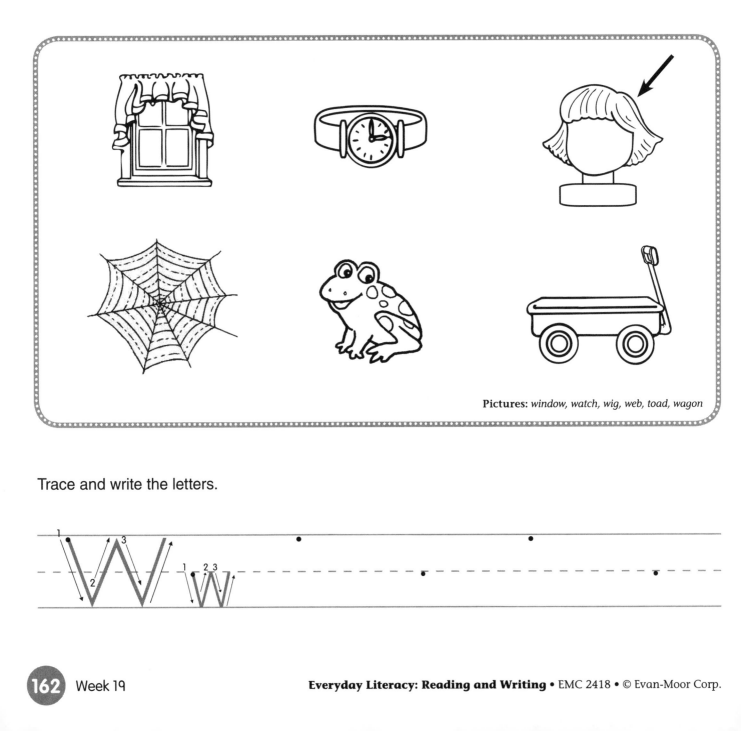

Pictures: *window, watch, wig, web, toad, wagon*

Trace and write the letters.

WEEK 20

Concept
Initial and Final Sounds:
H, P, W

Review It

Vocabulary
Words with _h_, _p_, or _w_ at the Beginning: horse, pig, walrus
Words with _p_ at the End: sheep
High-Frequency Words: a, are, big, is, little, that, you

Day 1

SKILLS:
Concepts of Print
- Identify uppercase and lowercase letters of the alphabet

Phonemic Awareness
- Isolate and identify the initial phoneme of a spoken word

Phonics/Word Analysis
- Recognize that individual letters have associated sounds

Writing
- Print uppercase and lowercase letters
- Use spacing between letters and words when writing on a line

I Know _Hh_, _Pp_, and _Ww_

Distribute the Day 1 activity and a writing tool to each student. Then say:

- _Point to the horse. What is the first sound in **horse**? (/h/) What letter stands for **/h/**? (H) Point to the uppercase **H**. Trace it. Now point to the lowercase **h**. Trace it. Now write two uppercase **H**s and two lowercase **h**'s on the line._

- _Point to the pig. What is the first sound in **pig**? (/p/) What letter stands for **/p/**? (P) Point to the uppercase **P**. Trace it. Now point to the lowercase **p**. Trace it. Now write two uppercase **P**s and two lowercase **p**'s on the line._

Repeat the process for the remaining picture and letters. Then direct students' attention to the next task. Say:

- _Look at the uppercase alphabet at the bottom of the page. Let's name the letters together._ (name aloud) _Circle uppercase **H**, **P**, and **W**._

- _Look at the lowercase alphabet below. Let's name the letters together._ (name aloud) _Now circle lowercase **h**, **p**, and **w**._

Day 1 activity

Day 2

SKILLS:
Phonemic Awareness
- Identify the position of an isolated phoneme in a spoken word

Phonics/Word Analysis
- Learn and apply letter-sound correspondences
- Recognize that individual letters have associated sounds
- Read familiar CVC words and common sight words

Listening for _Hh_, _Pp_, and _Ww_

Distribute the Day 2 activity and a writing tool to each student. Then say:

- _We are going to listen for letter sounds. Point to the **H** row. What sound does **H** stand for? (/h/) Say **hand**. (hand) Do you hear **/h/** first or last in **hand**? (first) Fill in the first circle under the hand. Say **house**. (house) Do you hear **/h/** first or last in **house**? (first) Fill in the first circle under the house. Say **hay**. (hay) Do you hear **/h/** first or last in **hay**? (first) Fill in the first circle._

- _Point to the **P** row. What sound does **P** stand for? (/p/) Say **pear**. (pear) Do you hear **/p/** first or last in **pear**? (first) Fill in the first circle. Say **cup**. (cup) Do you hear **/p/** first or last in **cup**? (last) Fill in the last circle. Say **map**. (map) Do you hear **/p/** first or last in **map**? (last) Fill in the last circle._

Repeat the process for the remaining letter and pictures. Then direct students' attention to the next task. Say:

- _Point to the sentence at the bottom of the page. Move your finger under each word as you read it aloud. Now fill in the circle beside the matching picture._

Day 2 activity

Day 3

SKILLS:

Concepts of Print
- Understand that spoken words are represented in writing by specific sequences of letters

Phonemic Awareness
- Isolate and identify the initial or final sound of a spoken word

Phonics/Word Analysis
- Learn and apply letter-sound correspondences
- Recognize that individual letters have associated sounds
- Read familiar CVC words and common sight words

Writing
- Write the letters that match sounds in words

Writing Words with *H, P,* and *W*

Distribute the Day 3 activity and a writing tool to each student. Say:

- *Each box shows a picture and a word that is missing a letter. We are going to say each picture name and write the missing letter. Point to the first picture. It shows a hen. Say* **hen**. *(hen) What is the first sound in* **hen**? *(/h/) Write the missing letter. Now move your finger under each letter as we read the word together:* **hen**.

- *Point to the picture in box 2. It shows a wig. Say* **wig**. *(wig) What is the first sound in* **wig**? *(/w/) Write the missing letter. Let's read the word together:* **wig**.

- *Point to the picture in box 3. What is it? (web) What is the first sound in* **web**? *(/w/) Write the missing letter. Let's read the word together:* **web**.

- *Point to the picture in box 4. It shows a cap. Say* **cap**. *(cap) What is the <u>last</u> sound in* **cap**? *(/p/) Write the missing letter. Let's read the word together:* **cap**.

- *Point to the picture in box 5. It shows hay. Say* **hay**. *(hay) What is the first sound in* **hay**? *(/h/) Write the missing letter. Let's read the word together:* **hay**.

- *Point to the picture in box 6. What is it? (pen) What is the first sound in* **pen**? *(/p/) Write the missing letter. Let's read the word together:* **pen**.

Day 3 activity

Day 4

SKILLS:

Phonics/Word Analysis
- Learn and apply letter-sound correspondences
- Read familiar CVC words and common sight words

Comprehension
- Demonstrate comprehension of text read aloud by self or others

Reading Words with *H, P,* and *W*

Distribute the Day 4 activity and pencils or crayons. Then say:

- *Point to the first sentence. Move your finger under the words as we read together:* **You are a big horse**. *Draw a line from this sentence to the picture it matches.*

- *Point to sentence 2. Move your finger under the words as we read together:* **You are a little horse**. *Draw a line from the sentence to the picture it matches.*

- *Point to sentence 3. Let's read it together:* **You are a big pig**. *Draw a line from the sentence to the picture it matches.*

- *Point to sentence 4. Let's read it together:* **You are a little sheep**. *Draw a line from the sentence to the picture it matches.*

- *Point to sentence 5. Let's read it together:* **You are a big walrus**. *Draw a line from the sentence to the picture it matches.*

- *Point to the last sentence. Write a word to complete the sentence. Then draw a picture that matches what you wrote.*

Day 4 activity

SKILLS:
Phonemic Awareness

• Isolate and identify the initial or final phoneme of a spoken word

Phonics/Word Analysis

• Learn and apply letter-sound correspondences

• Recognize that individual letters have associated sounds

Home–School Connection p. 170
Spanish version available (see p. 2)

Phonics Review Game

Play the following game to review the initial and final consonant sounds that students have learned this week.

Materials: 6 large index cards or 3 sheets of construction paper cut in half

Preparation: Write the letter **h** on two cards, the letter **p** on two cards, and the letter **w** on two cards. Divide the cards into two sets that contain one of each letter. Display one set of cards on each end of the board.

How to Play: Divide students into two teams. Have each team line up facing the board. Explain to students that you will say a word and that they should listen for the beginning sound. After you say the word, the first player in each line races up to the board, chooses the correct letter card, faces his or her team, and says the letter name aloud. Each correct answer is worth one point. The two players then return the cards to the ledge and go to the end of the line. Repeat the process until you have called all of the words in the chart below. The team with the most points wins. Play the game again, and have students listen for ending sounds.

Beginning Sounds:	Ending Sounds:
H: horn, hand, hay, horse	**H:** none
P: pear, pig, pen, pie	**P:** drip, cap, cup, sheep
W: water, web, walrus, watch	**W:** none

Name _____

Write It!

Trace then write each letter.

Find uppercase **H**, **P**, and **W**. Circle them.

A	B	C	D	E	F	G	H	I	J	K	L	M
N	O	P	Q	R	S	T	U	V	W	X	Y	Z

Find lowercase **h**, **p**, and **w**. Circle them.

a	b	c	d	e	f	g	h	i	j	k	l	m
n	o	p	q	r	s	t	u	v	w	x	y	z

Name _____

Listen for It!

Where do you hear the letter sound?
Fill in the circle to show **first** or **last**.

Read the sentence.
Fill in the circle next to the correct picture.

That is a big pig.

Name _____

Spell It!

Say each picture name.
Write the missing letter.

h p w

1

___ en

2

___ ig

3

___ eb

4

ca ___

5

___ ay

6

___ en

Everyday Literacy: Reading and Writing • EMC 2418 • © Evan-Moor Corp.

Name _____

Read It!

Read the sentence.
Draw a line to the correct picture.

1 You are a big horse.

2 You are a little horse.

3 You are a big pig.

4 You are a little sheep.

5 You are a big walrus.

Complete the sentence.
Draw a picture to match.

You are a little _____.

Name _____

Beginning and Ending
Hh Pp Ww

WEEK 20

Home–School Connection

To Parents

This week your child reviewed beginning and ending sounds for the letters **H**, **P**, and **W**.

Name each picture. Draw a line to show what letter sound you hear at the **beginning**.

 •

 •

 •

p

W

h

Pictures: *window, pear, hand*

Name each picture. Circle the picture that **ends** with the sound of **P**.

Pictures: *hen, dog, sheep*

Hh

Pp

Ww

Everyday Literacy: Reading and Writing • EMC 2418 • © Evan-Moor Corp.

Answer Key

Week 1

Day 1

Day 2

Day 3

Day 4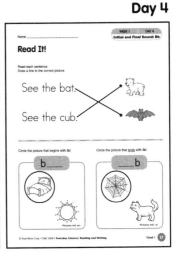

Week 2

Day 1

Day 2

Day 3

Day 4

Week 3

Day 1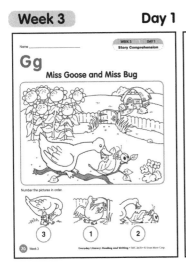

Day 2

Day 3

Day 4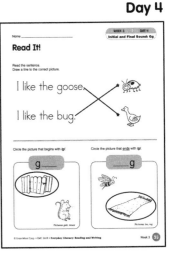

Week 4   Day 1   Day 2   Day 3   Day 4

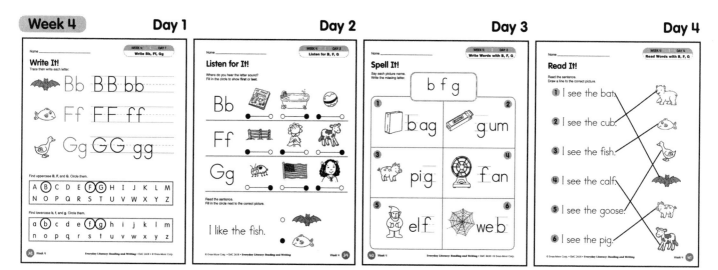

Week 5   Day 1   Day 2   Day 3   Day 4

Week 6   Day 1   Day 2   Day 3   Day 4

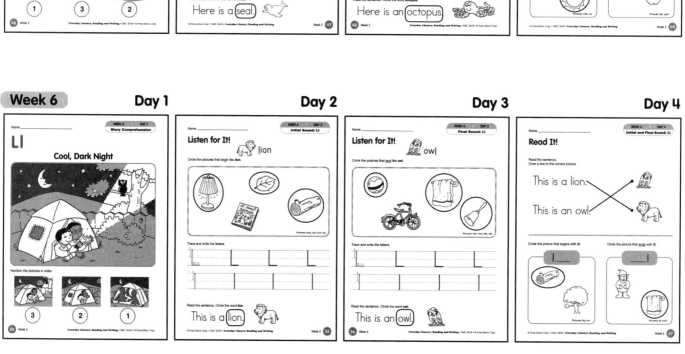

Week 7 Day 1 Day 2 Day 3 Day 4

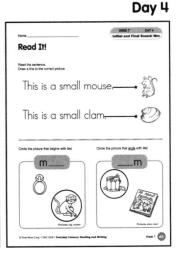

Week 8 Day 1 Day 2 Day 3 Day 4

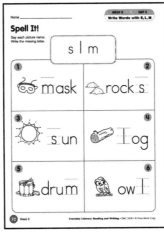
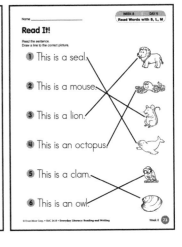

Week 9 Day 1 Day 2 Day 3 Day 4

Week 10   Day 1   Day 2   Day 3   Day 4

Week 11   Day 1   Day 2   Day 3   Day 4

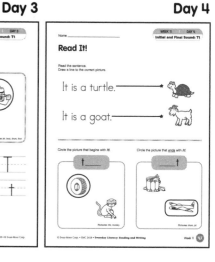

Week 12   Day 1   Day 2   Day 3   Day 4

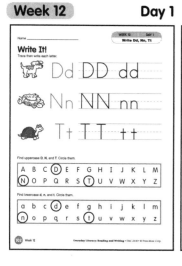

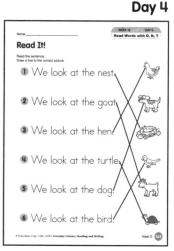

Everyday Literacy: Reading and Writing • EMC 2418 • © Evan-Moor Corp.

Week 13

Day 1

Day 2

Day 3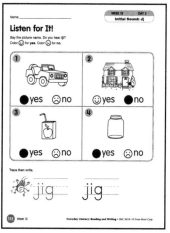

Day 4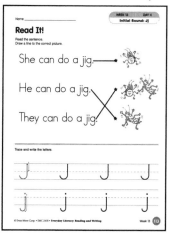

Week 14

Day 1

Day 2

Day 3

Day 4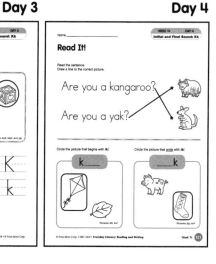

Week 15

Day 1

Day 2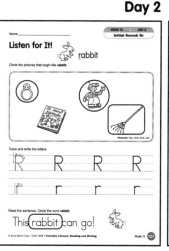

Day 3

Day 4

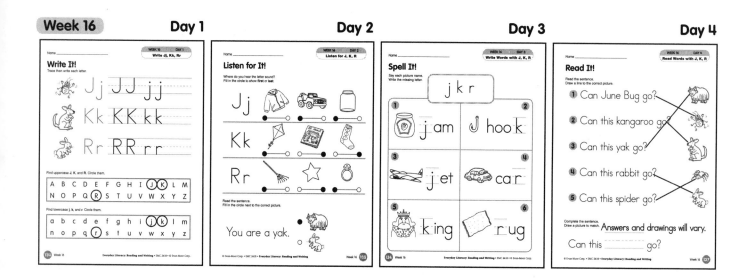

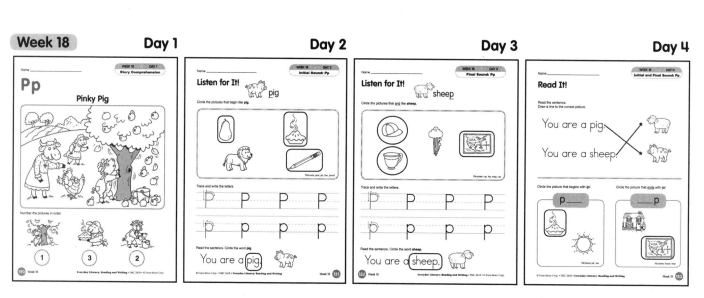